T0021689

Alzheimer's Through the Alphabet

One Journey of Ups and Downs

LESLIE F. HERGERT

ARCHWAY
PUBLISHING

Archway Publishing books may be ordered
through booksellers or by contacting:

Archway Publishing
1663 Liberty Drive
Bloomington, IN 47403
www.archwaypublishing.com
1 (888) 242-5904

ISBN: 978-1-4808-5964-7 (sc)
ISBN: 978-1-4808-5965-4 (e)

Library of Congress Control Number: 2018902220

Print information available on the last page.

Archway Publishing rev. date: 03/16/2018

Contents

Introduction

Memoirs about living with Alzheimer's typically have no happy ending. Because Alzheimer's is progressive and incurable, people fear it and avoid those who have it. But don't we all in some way have a similar experience? We all live, and we all will die. Like most of life, the Alzheimer's journey is not really a downhill slide but more a jumble of events and feelings that shift from moment to moment. As one Alzheimer's caregiver said about her week, "You know, we laughed, we cried, we yelled—pretty normal week!" I have chosen an ABC format to try to capture these ups and downs and the variety of experiences at each and every stage of the Alzheimer's journey.

While people dealing with Alzheimer's share many experiences, each individual is unique and has a different journey. Sometimes onset is quick and dramatic, but most times little problems appear and then get worse until it is obvious something is very wrong. Sometimes people with Alzheimer's change and become more aggressive or more docile than they have been; sometimes their personality remains visible even as their capacities decrease. Some people have lots of support; some become quite isolated. Some people lose their abilities to a certain point and then die somewhat abruptly; others live for a long time in a liminal state, somewhere between life and death.

The story I tell here is the story of one person and one family, which is both similar to and different from other stories about people with Alzheimer's. We are and have been extremely lucky and blessed along this journey. That is one way our story is different from others. Though not rich, we have had sufficient financial resources, between our own money and access to public support. We are extremely rich in terms of family and friend supports. We have not suffered from violence or other hardships, and we have found excellent care facilities when we needed then. We live in an urban area in a city and state that cares and provides for its vulnerable citizens, including the elderly and disabled; we are not geographically isolated, and there are many resources available. We recognize that for many people, this will be a story of privilege.

This narrative provides little, if any, advice. I recognize that my way may not be your way. I hope some of the experiences described here spark ideas for ways of coping or suggest resources that might be available. I hope people living with or caring for people with dementia will find comfort in knowing they are not alone and that the journey is full of joys as well as sorrows, fun as well as difficulties.

Let me first introduce the main characters in our story. My husband, Ralph, is now in the end stages of Alzheimer's and living in a very nice nursing home. Ralph, who was born in 1946, was in his late fifties when things started to fall apart. He was diagnosed with "probable early-onset Alzheimer's" when he was sixty-two. We have been married for fifty years. We met in VISTA, the domestic Peace Corps, in 1966 and married six months after we met—but that's another story!

Ralph was bivocational, combining work as a Christian minister with public-service work. I have always worked full time and, during the period described here had a demanding but flexible job that required a fair amount of national and international travel. We have one adult daughter Jesse, who lived and worked in New York City for several years before moving back to Massachusetts when Ralph's disease began to progress. She has provided constant and loving support.

Ralph and I lived in a two-family house in Somerville, for many years with my mother downstairs. At the time of most of the events described here, my mother was in her late eighties and early nineties—mentally sharp but visually impaired and with numerous health problems. She lived independently in her own apartment downstairs from us, kept up with friends and family, and volunteered at Mount Auburn Hospital until she died in 2013 at the age of ninety-four. After that, Jesse moved into her apartment.

My family lives in Massachusetts; Ralph's is in California. The other important characters in our story are our home church, Old Cambridge Baptist Church (OCBC) in Harvard Square, and the Alzheimer's Association, whose early-onset/early-stage support group and resources were very important to us.

Ralph was a lively and lovely man, committed to doing good in the world and having a really good time doing it (as E. B. White said). He was a Baptist minister and city official in our home city of Somerville for over ten years, and for his entire career he combined work in the church and work in the community. He was a conscientious objector—to war in general and the Vietnam War in particular—and did his alternate service driving a Bloodmobile for the Red Cross. He was extremely smart but relatable and popular in many very different circles. He was a preacher and an activist, a political progressive and a Christian. His faith was somewhat traditional, but he believed that, as a button he wore said, "God is Love is the only theology I need." He was friends with politicians and highly educated people, and he knew every street person in Somerville.

In the early 2000s, it became clear that something was wrong with Ralph. He could not focus, experienced numerous problems at work, and lost his city job in 2001. The small church he pastored (not OCBC) was losing members and moving toward closure, so we thought the two career losses were contributing to depression. We sought a variety of "cures," but while he often seemed okay, at other times he did not. In 2005, an incident occurred that to me was dramatic and prompted me to more aggressively seek help, ultimately getting to the Brigham and Women's Alzheimer's Center. In 2009, he was diagnosed with probable Alzheimer's (more about this under "Doctors and Diagnosis"). In 2014, he entered a nursing home, and by 2015, he was unable to stand, speak, or feed himself. In 2017, he is still living in the nursing home.

But that is jumping ahead. This story is not chronological but a jumble of experiences, feelings, and thoughts—some tangible, some happy, some sad. Feel free to read *Alzheimer's through the Alphabet* in order or to jump around and read whatever strikes your fancy or might meet an interest or need. If you read the book from front to back, you may find events out of order. (A timeline is included at the end as an appendix.) If you start to get too sad, read "Laughter"! I start by describing "Activities" and what Ralph could and couldn't do in the early stages. But "Doctors and Diagnosis" comes after "Activities," and some topics include feelings at every stage.

The Alzheimer's Alphabet

Activities

For several years after losing his primary jobs in the city and the church, Ralph continued to work, albeit at progressively—or regressively—limited jobs. When he stopped being able to handle professional jobs, he took a part-time job making phone calls for Barack Obama's presidential campaign. Then he had to stop working altogether.

Ralph needed to find things to do that suited his changing capacities. He felt bad about not working, so he did household chores like cleaning and laundry for a few years as his contribution to our family. This was important to him and much appreciated by me. (Some people complain about the way their spouses do household tasks, but I have low standards, so I was thrilled!)

The church he pastored had closed, so he rejoined our "home church" Old Cambridge Baptist Church and became active in committees and the choir. He went for walks, both alone and with friends. He found he loved to sing, so friends helped him join a singing group for people with Parkinson's: the Tremble Clefs! He tried out for and appeared in the Christmas Revels, a local singing and dancing production for the winter solstice, and he was able to learn all the music for a two-hour production.

Among the other people we knew with Alzheimer's, Eric, who

had been an engineer, became a bagger at the local supermarket, riding his bike to work and becoming popular with employees and customers, while Bob, who was very athletic, rode his bike and swam with friends or paid companions for several years. Other people engaged in old and new hobbies, such as learning to paint and using carpentry skills to make tables. Spouses, other relatives, or friends who did not work took their partners to various local activities at senior centers and libraries.

I searched for activities for Ralph to do and reduced my work time so I was home one day a week. Through the Alzheimer's Association, we participated together in an early-onset/early-stage support group, and through that group, we found some activities that Ralph could do without me, including trips to museums with trained guides and art appreciation programs. The Boston University Medical School Buddies program paired people with early-stage Alzheimer's with first-year medical students. Ralph had a series of young people once a month for four years. They walked the neighborhood where Ralph knew everyone, visited local museums, and went out for coffee. Several were beautiful young women, and my hairdresser would say, "I saw Ralph with his girlfriend last week!"

We also took on Alzheimer's as a hobby (well, that's what I called it!), speaking at various events about the disease and raising money through the Walk to End Alzheimer's. (Our support group's team was called the Unforgettables.) One year, we were part of several media events. We recorded our story through Story Corps; Ralph was featured on WBUR and NPR in a four-part "day in the life of someone with Alzheimer's;" and we were part of the first *Reason to Hope* video for the local Alzheimer's Association. At that point, I googled myself and found my professional online presence had been replaced by what I started to call "Leslie, the Alzheimer's chick." I decided not to worry about that, as I knew I was looking at retirement in just a few years and my professional life was coming to a close anyway.

Writing this now, it seems like we—Ralph in particular—were very active. But at the time, there were a lot of hours to fill with things to keep Ralph busy. It was tricky finding the right activities and the supports he needed to participate in them (see "Juggling"). He needed help finding activities he could do on his own, scheduling and remembering what was scheduled, and arranging transportation. There were some activities he could do if he could get there, if he was watched all the time, or if he was helped with some aspect. I could not find many of these, and the support he needed changed over time. For example, for a while he could drive, and then he couldn't.

Today, there are many more activities in the community geared to people with early-stage Alzheimer's; the Alzheimer's Association lists many, as do local councils on aging and other elder service groups. The "memory cafés" that are springing up would have been perfect for Ralph.

At some point, I became uncomfortable with leaving him alone all day, and he became frustrated by the things he could not do. I suggested we look into day programs. He was somewhat resistant at first. "I'm okay at home," he said, "and I don't think I need anything like that."

I had heard about Rogerson House, and a friend of his from our support group was going there. "Let's just visit and see what it's like," I suggested. "Willie is there, you know."

So we went and found a beautiful old house on the Jamaicaway, surrounded by trees and across from Jamaica Pond. Inside was a comfortable living room, and upstairs, past coded elevators and doors, was the room for program participants. The room was sunny and cheerful, with different areas set up for different activities. But what we could see most clearly was a group of old ladies doing crafts. *Uh oh!* I thought. *Ralph is not going to respond well to that.* And I wondered how he would get there, as it was time-consuming to get from Somerville to Jamaica Plain, especially in the rush hour.

See "Day Program" for how things turned out.

Annoying Period

Here is a fact most of us do not admit when talking about Alzheimer's: our loved ones with Alzheimer's do lots of annoying things, like repeating questions and comments; losing things; losing things and thinking someone stole them; and putting things in odd places (like the keys in the freezer). When Ralph was still working and had not yet been diagnosed, his car broke down in a town about thirty miles from home. He called me at work twenty times in an hour (I kept track after the first five). Finally, I left work and went to pick him up.

Another time, after he was diagnosed, we were driving to Maine and Ralph asked, "Where are we going?" several times in a few hours. The first few times I just answered the question. Then I tried to use a technique someone described in our support group: answering the question in a different way each time he asked. This might not have been the best for him, but it was entertaining for me! Then I just got annoyed.

At one point in our early-stage support group, I described this as "the annoying period." Yes, someone said, but it will only get worse from here. That is true. But even as it gets worse, it does not get more annoying. It gets sadder, scarier, and more frustrating, but not more annoying. It would be good if we could appreciate this time as the period when we can still communicate and connect, but I think most of us will just get annoyed and move on.

B

Becoming a Better Person

Shortly after Ralph was diagnosed, after some years of difficulties, I decided that this crisis would give me an opportunity to "become a better person." I said it as a joke (at least, people always laughed when I said it!), but here is my confession: I actually meant it. I felt bad that I had been yelling at Ralph a lot for the past few years, thinking he wasn't paying attention, should try harder, etc. I had periods of sympathy and support, and I made sure we explored many possible diagnoses and treatments, such as depression, sleep apnea, and different jobs. But then I would get fed up and start yelling.

In truth, this was not new behavior. Basically, in our

relationship, I was often a bitch and Ralph was Saint Ralph. I lost my temper a lot, and I was bossy and critical. With the Alzheimer's diagnosis, I saw that much of my behavior had been unfair and rude. While there were times when I had good reason to be annoyed and even angry, I could have been more accepting and let some things go.

Over the many years of our marriage, I had seen Ralph's good qualities and weaknesses, as well as my own. I had admired his work, his role as a father, and his kindness to so many people. I had even started to accept his shortcomings because I could recognize and appreciate the fact that he seemed to accept mine. This Alzheimer's thing would give me the opportunity to become more patient, more accepting, more loving, and more kind.

Well, that was the goal.

C

Care

Care means different things at different stages of the disease. In the early stage, the Alzheimer's Association uses the term "care partner" because people with the disease can continue to function in many areas and may just need specific supports. This varies dramatically from person to person, and within a couple, the two people may differ in how they interpret the role. So one care partner may try to help while the person with the disease does not feel he or she needs the help.

As an organization consultant, I was taught it's not *help* if the person being helped doesn't see it as help. But that rule doesn't work with Alzheimer's. Some people with the disease think they are fine while their partners see that they are in danger of some kind—whether from physical risk or embarrassment. At this stage, the care partner's role is one of support, enabling the partner to be as active as possible for as long as possible and to do this tactfully and subtly. Care may include arranging activities, driving the partner to activities, rearranging the house, and creating organizational supports.

Because Alzheimer's is a progressive disease, care becomes more direct over time. For a while, Ralph could drive alone; then he drove only with me in the car giving him directions; and then

I drove. He could dress himself; then I helped him choose clothes; then I helped him put on his shoes and pants; and then I buttoned his shirts and put on his belt.

Now that Ralph is in a nursing home, my care is limited. I choose to go at lunchtime so I have something to do: feed him lunch. Others at the nursing home take their spouse for a walk or read newspapers to their friend. There is little to do at a good nursing home, which may be why some visitors actively complain so much—complaining gives them something to do to care for their loved ones and advocate for them.

The typical caregiver/care partner is either a spouse or the adult child of a parent with Alzheimer's. But in our support group, there were brothers and sisters, a brother-in-law, and neighbors of a nun. In the nursing home, in addition to spouses and children, I see a variety of regular visitors: friends, a sister, a longtime lover who is not a spouse. Two of our close friends regularly visit Ralph, which sometimes gives me a day off (really helpful when I was working and really nice now that I'm not) and sometimes provides me with company and support as they care for me as much as for Ralph.

Communication

Communication was always one of Ralph's great talents. He was smart, warm, funny, and could communicate with a wide range of people. His city and church jobs brought him into contact with street people, some of whom were crazy; city and state officials, some of whom were crazy; and a wide range of others. Once, I hosted a cocktail party at our house for a work group of educators from around the country, which included a federal program officer who oversaw the federal grant we were working on. The Fed was notoriously difficult to work with, and I got nervous as the evening approached. Ralph won him over immediately with stories about being a cab driver (he was in divinity school then, driving a cab on the side), which the federal program officer said was the favorite job he'd ever had.

Dinner at our house was always full of conversation. Even when Ralph had jobs with lots of night meetings, he always came home for dinner with me and our daughter, Jesse, even with a thirty-minute commute. We each told about our day, and that was often enough to spark other conversation. A friend who stayed with us after her divorce said, "So this is what people talk about at dinner." We didn't understand what she meant.

Once, Jesse, age five, asked a question that Ralph took to have theological import. He answered with a long dissertation. I tried to interrupt but stopped when I saw her nodding her little head while she looked at her father seriously. When he finally did stop talking, Jesse said, "That was very interesting, Dad. I didn't understand any of it, but it was very interesting."

In the early stages of the disease, Ralph began to be less articulate and to forget what he had just said, but he could cover it up pretty quickly and still was capable of making social conversation. Even well into the disease, he was charming and outgoing in various social settings like church and parties, even with people he did not know well. He could cover mistakes, and he used humor and hugs to maneuver through a variety of situations.

After he was in the nursing home, he had two seizures that left him unable to walk and with very little ability to speak. He would say a few words here and there, often in greeting me and Jesse, and sometimes even with friends. From time to time, he would smile in response to someone or something, and his smile lit his face in a way that reminded me of the way he used to be.

About six months after he entered the nursing home, our church choir went to sing for him, and he was thrilled. His face lit up; he said, "What a guy!" to our friend Keene; and he even sang a bit of some of the songs he knew. Some months later, when his verbal ability really went missing, he would often make eye contact and smile at family and friends who visited, and he would make faces and wiggle his eyebrows, just to be funny. It makes me smile just remembering that.

A year ago, he looked me in the eyes—it had been a very long time since that had happened—and said, "Wonderful!" That was the last thing he said to me, and I hold on to that.

With some other nursing home residents, I have semifake conversations. I do not understand what they are saying, but I respond with a smile and a sentence in the same tone of voice they are using. I ask a question and nod when they answer. They smile back at me, and we are both happily engaged.

One woman constantly asks her daughter, "Are you my sister? Are you my daughter?" It drives the daughter crazy, and for a while I thought, "Well, at least she is trying to communicate with you. Ralph can't communicate at all." Then I decided that was glib and judgmental—even though I never said it out loud. When Ralph used to ask the same thing over and over, it drove me batty (see "Annoying Period"). I understand why people might think there is no point in visiting when there is no longer any communication and their loved one does not know them.

When I visit Ralph, I wonder how to communicate with him. It has now been over a year since he has communicated in any way. He does not smile much, although from time to time he laughs as he wakes up from a nap. He is not able to speak at all. He rarely makes eye contact with me or anyone else. While I feed him, I tell him about my day and news from friends and family. Jesse and I rub his hands and arms, we kiss his forehead, we sing to him. But none of this elicits any response that I can tell.

Jesse and some of the aides do not agree with this description. They say he does respond to us, and they point to the way he communicates his preferences about his food. He keeps his mouth shut when he is not ready for another spoonful, and he opens it when he wants more. He sometimes looks uncomfortable for a while, and then his face relaxes, maybe in response to our touch. Sometimes, when he is waking up from a nap, he smiles just a little bit. Maybe the communication at this point comes in microcommunications that I need to learn to notice and appreciate. Does he hear and understand some things but is not able to respond? Or is nothing going on inside his brain?

What is communication anyway? Is it enough to just be present? For a person to feel your touch and see a loving face? Sometimes I think of babies, who cannot talk back when you talk to them. However, the situation is really different, since a baby responds to a voice and a loving touch, making noises back to the adult—noises that gradually begin to make sense. Ralph does not respond or responds in minimal ways. I think it is important to be with him and for him to feel a loving touch, but I don't know whether it is communication. Nevertheless, I hold his hand and tell him things about my day and try to remember the dinner conversations we used to have.

D

Doctors and Diagnosis

Diagnosing Alzheimer's is difficult because its symptoms can be symptoms of many other things, like depression or even dehydration.

Ralph lost his city job in 2001 after an incident we now think was an early sign of his dementia, although he was not diagnosed until 2009. For three or four years after losing his job, he struggled to find and keep jobs. We were told by doctors that he had depression and sleep apnea, both of which were treated, but symptoms continued. Finally, in 2005, he experienced several instances of forgetting discussions we had literally had five minutes earlier and losing track of Zipcars he had rented.

I was becoming seriously concerned and took him back to his primary care physician, who insisted nothing was wrong—"He's just getting older"—but did agree to send him for testing. The three hours of testing showed that, as the doctor told us, "He only has mild cognitive impairment." I did not know, nor did the doctor tell us, that this category can be an early stage of dementia. We were assured that it was a sign of his depression.

In 2006, Ralph and I went to Italy with another couple. Maria had been a college roommate of mine, and she and her husband,

David, had become friends of ours. However, we had never traveled together.

We had a wonderful time. We rented a car, and David drove us everywhere because Ralph had forgotten to make the arrangements that would let him drive the rental car. We didn't think anything of that at the time. But after the trip, Maria asked me to have lunch with her. She told me that she and David had noticed Ralph becoming extremely anxious when he was not with me. I had noticed a little of this but didn't want to hover, so from time to time I went into stores alone after making sure that one of our friends was near. Maria told me that they noticed Ralph's anxiety enough that they made sure one of them was with him if I wasn't around. Maria's mother had Alzheimer's, and she was giving me a gentle warning.

Another year of treatment for depression and sleep apnea went by with increasing incidents of forgetfulness and poor judgment. However, Ralph did not seem all that depressed by this time—more upset when these incidents occurred.

One day, in early 2007, I became distraught at work, and a friend put me in touch with his friend who is a nationally known expert in Alzheimer's disease. This doctor asked me to send him a description of what was going on and then called me on a Sunday afternoon and talked with me for forty-five minutes, asking diagnostic questions. He finally said that Ralph's particular test results were unlikely to be due to depression, although one could be depressed because of losing capacity. He recommended that we go to the Brigham and Women's Memory Disorder Group, which provides a coordinated set of diagnosis and treatment from different fields of expertise.

Because we needed a referral, we went back to our primary care physician, who sent us to a neurologist. I raised my concerns without asking directly for a referral at first. Both doctors were dismissive of my concerns and treated me like an overly protective spouse whom they were tolerating. At one point, the neurologist said they had "ruled out dementia" and threw an article at me to show that these concerns were natural and normal for a "man of his age." Ralph had just turned sixty.

"But," he said finally, "if you really want to, I can refer you to Brigham and Women's."

I said, "Yes, please."

We went to the Brigham and started a year of testing with doctors from different specialties who coordinated their work. It took more than a year before Ralph was finally diagnosed with "probable Alzheimer's. But during that time, we were treated respectfully and referred to resources, including the Alzheimer's Association. We were able to start attending a support group at the Alzheimer's Association even before Ralph was formally diagnosed in 2009.

Because this disease is difficult to diagnose and affects different people differently, it is essential that doctors, especially primary care physicians, be trained to know what to look for and how to deal with people who come to them with concerns. They need to be taught how to listen carefully to patients' concerns and coordinate treatment of different symptoms. Doctors need to be able to recommend diagnostic tests beyond simple fifteen-minute questions in an office and understand how to interpret results. And they need to be able to communicate results with their patients clearly, honestly, and with respect for the difficult journey their patients are beginning.

Day Program

Ralph did not go from diagnosis into a day program. As I described in "Activities," he was able to keep active at home for three or four years. But as his disease progressed, I worried that he was bored and potentially unsafe being alone for so many hours. We heard good things about Rogerson House in our support group, but when we first visited, he said, "I don't think this is for me. I don't need that. I am fine at home on my own."

Not really, I thought.

While my mother was alive, she and Ralph checked on each other and kind of helped each other. But I was working, and as Ralph was able to do less and less, I worried about all kinds of problems Ralph could have in the many hours he was alone. I also traveled for work and was afraid of leaving him then too, although he and my mother took care of each other. So I tried to talk him into the day program.

"It'll be like camp," I said, knowing that he and I had had positive experiences working in a Girl Scout camp together. Finally, I told him to just give it a try for a week and if he didn't like it, he didn't have to go back. That was a lie, but it worked for him. He went, he enjoyed being with people, and he forgot he thought he wouldn't like it.

It turned out there were not just old ladies doing crafts but a men's group that discussed current events; a group that wrote poetry together; and several activities he enjoyed, like music and drumming. He connected with one staff person who knew someone he knew and another staff person who would take him on long walks around Jamaica Pond. He often related to the staff and "helped" with older people or people who were more disabled. He had a good time there, and I didn't worry about him all day.

We were lucky to live in an area that has The Ride—a public reduced-fare taxi service for people with disabilities—so he got picked up and dropped off, and I really had coverage for nearly a full day of work.

I was surprised at several things the day program revealed about changes in Ralph. The sex segregation was the first. Ralph had often worked predominantly with women, as he worked in social services as a day care teacher, a church pastor, etc. Even in his city job, his staff were mostly women, and he was the person the few women police officers came to with problems on the job. But at Rogerson House, he was solidly in the "men's group."

He had always loved small children, at one point working in day care. Once a week, a day care program came to visit with toddlers and their parents. I was surprised when the staff told me Ralph had no interest in that and always chose a different activity. Alzheimer's affects many aspects of life, and I learned not to say, "Ralph likes this" or doesn't like that.

Early Onset

Most people think of Alzheimer's as an old person's disease. We expect it in old people. It is normal to lose track of things, to forget things, and to change personality when you are old. After all, it used to be called *senility*. But having these difficulties when you are young is unexpected, which is one reason Alzheimer's is hard to diagnose.

Our early-onset support group, for people diagnosed with Alzheimer's before age sixty-five, included some people who were in their late forties and early fifties. Some had teenage children. Many had to stop working earlier than they wanted or needed to be able to support themselves.

Early-onset Alzheimer's brings a raft of challenges. People may not be able to support themselves and/or their family, and they may not qualify for some subsidies available for older people. Those who are big and strong, usually men, may react physically to frustrations, endangering family members and becoming frightening and hard to deal with. In nursing homes, men's beds are often in short supply, and administrators may not be willing to take the risk of dealing with aggressive behavior.

It is hard to lose dreams of moving into old age together. Ralph and I were not the kind of people who postponed things—trips, activities—until retirement. Neither of us had a bucket list. But Ralph's grandfather had lived into his nineties, marrying a new wife in his eighties. I expected Ralph to do the same!

We did not have children at home to care for or the kind of responsibilities many others have. We did not rely on Ralph's salary. But I did think we would spend our old age together, walking around holding hands the way we used to see Julia Child and her husband, Paul, walking in the neighborhood. We had not put off traveling, but I always assumed we would do more together, driving the country to visit friends. (In my fantasies, Ralph would be driving.) We would be companions, enjoying each other's company.

Early-onset Alzheimer's cuts short whatever plans and expectations one has for the future. For people younger than we were, it comes *in media res*, in the middle of life, just at a time when people are juggling children, parents, jobs, and other responsibilities. It is unexpected and harder to deal with.

End of the World

A diagnosis of Alzheimer's feels like the end of the world, and it is. But at the same time, it isn't. It definitely is the end of the world you have lived in and the expectations you had for the future. Most people fear such a diagnosis and avoid it because of that fear. They fear what they have heard, and they fear the end of the person they or their loved one has been.

But after a while, you realize that you have just entered a different world—one with new challenges, new people, new routines, and yes, new joys, if you can pay attention to them. The Alzheimer's journey may be long or short, may be more or less difficult, but you can endure it, you can bear it, and you can live with it. You may need a lot of help and support—I certainly did— and you can find that help in a variety of places.

When Ralph was finally diagnosed with probable Alzheimer's, one of the doctors said, "Welcome to the family." I was not especially happy to hear that at the time, but I came to realize that we *had* joined a new family, one that would support us in the new world we had entered. It was good to know that there were guides and fellow travelers—people to welcome us and help us navigate the journey.

Fear

I have already written (in "Doctors and Diagnosis") about the period when it was clear that something was really wrong with Ralph and the difficulty in getting a diagnosis. I have not written enough about the fear and panic I felt during this period (which stretched on for four or five years). We were resourceful in seeking help—well, I was insistent and Ralph went along with me—and explored multiple diagnoses and "cures," from depression and therapy to sleep apnea and the mask. I vacillated between yelling in frustration over things Ralph did that I labeled "thoughtless" to loving acceptance of his foibles and shortcomings.

What I did not acknowledge—what I tried to avoid in all the activity—was the fear I felt. What is going on? How can we handle this? How long will this problem last? What does the future hold for us?

While some people have a clearer sense that they are facing Alzheimer's or some other kind of dementia, we didn't think of that for years. It was not part of our family history, so it was not something we worried about. (Or maybe I just don't remember having that fear.) Whatever it was, however, it became clear over time that *something* was very wrong.

I was reminded of this panic recently when I talked with

several people facing early problems or a round of testing. I could feel their panic.

"How could this happen? She was fine yesterday."

"He won't acknowledge there is anything wrong. How can we take care of things if he won't admit there's a problem?"

People often see Alzheimer's as their worst fear and avoid confirming it. It is easy to explain problems away because it is true that everyone forgets things, loses track of where they were, screws up their checkbook … sometimes. It is difficult to say what is "normal" and what isn't.

As the problems pile up or get worse or cause other problems in life, the fear piles up too and becomes harder to ignore. Maybe that is why the diagnosis often seems like a relief. The uncertainty is gone, and now we can get on with dealing with this new reality.

Friends and Family

We were blessed with support from both family and friends, which we know is not true for everyone. Our daughter, Jesse, was living in New York at the time but moved to the Boston area when she recognized that things were starting to get more difficult. It was good to have her close, and she was always a great support. After my mother died in 2013, Jesse moved into my mother's apartment downstairs, and I was so grateful for that when Ralph had the breakdown that led to his final hospitalization and ultimate nursing home move. Jesse goes with me to visit Ralph on both Saturdays and Sundays every week, which is good company and a great support.

Both our extended families—mine in Massachusetts and Ralph's in California—supported our decisions and provided what help they could. For years, Ralph's brother Dennis called Ralph every Monday morning as he drove to work. Ralph really enjoyed those phone visits. Ralph's mother, Earline, pulled me aside the last time we visited to say, "I know you are caring for

Ralph and making the best decisions for him. We love you and trust you." I cannot stress enough how much this meant to me. Many people we know had struggles with family members about their decisions. No one but the closest caregiver can know what needs are appearing and how much they can handle. I really think that supporting my decisions was the best support our families gave. In addition, several of my family members visited Ralph in the nursing home periodically.

Friends are important to me, although I am not a very good friend. I don't call people enough or keep in touch very well. I am very sporadic about sending birthday cards. I tend to be close and personal with people I work with but not very good about keeping up with them after I leave. Ralph was even worse—he was a "love the one you're with" guy because of his navy upbringing. (He attended fourteen schools before college.) He made friends fast and then moved on to the next posting. Alzheimer's has made us grateful for the close friends we have and introduced us to new friends in new categories.

Longtime Friends

These are the people most people would consider friends. We do things together, and we talk either by phone or in person (although not that much). Many of our closest friends are part of our church community—see the next category. Some used to be part of Old Cambridge Baptist Church (OCBC) and then moved or joined another church or stopped going to church. Some used to be work friends of Ralph's. Some I see often, others not. Some call to check in, and others help in specific ways.

Church Community

We started going to OCBC in 1970, so most of our close friends are there. We attended together for several years before Ralph began pastoring other churches, first as a substitute preacher and then for about fifteen years in his own church. When his church closed and he was in the earliest stages of Alzheimer's, he returned to OCBC and began singing in the choir and participating in committees.

Being part of a church community was a blessing and a support. Ralph announced his Alzheimer's openly so everyone knew about it. Church members signed up to take Ralph for walks (see "Supports") and helped him participate in church activities as he was able. One team he was on asked him to lead prayers, and two basses in the choir helped Ralph find the right page of music, making it possible for him to sing longer than he might have been able to without their help. When he got lost (see "Walkabout"), the pastor and a friend showed up at our house with coffee and laptops, sending out calls to the whole community to watch for him and keeping me company. I would never have asked. Being in a community has made a huge difference to our lives.

Support Group Friends

Many of the people in our early-stage support group became important friends. I am not comfortable "whining" about my troubles with even close friends. In the support group, however, we share our trials and tribulations, successes and funny stories (some of which I wrote down and include here). Our support group includes women and men from different walks of life; some I would never have crossed paths with. We were joined by a common experience and a common attitude and approach to dealing with it: feisty and funny. Some people came and went—I guess the ones who didn't have the same attitude! Our support group was the best. We laughed and cried with each other, had parties together where we played games and danced, and went to each other's loved one's funerals.

It has been sad to lose touch with people as they move on to new phases of their lives. I still keep in touch with one friend, and another just called me after a year or so. They hold a special place in my heart.

Nursing Home Friends

Some regular visitors in the nursing home have become like work friends. Pauline was the best. She came every day to help her husband with lunch (fitting the visit in between her job driving a van of special needs kids to school) and had been doing that for over fifteen years. She had that feisty and funny attitude and was also a bundle of energy.

When her husband died and she stopped coming, there was a palpable difference in the dining room. I felt a deep loss, even though we do stay in touch. There are other people we eat with in the dining room or outside on nice summer days, and we all find it more fun to be together than being alone with loved ones who communicate with difficulty or not at all. But you have to get used to the fact that people die in a nursing home and your "friends" disappear.

Fading

One of the difficult things about this disease is that the person with Alzheimer's disappears over time, a little at a time. That time can be short or go on for many years, but the losses pile on over that period as you experience each loss, get used to it, and then get hit with another.

Ralph was a vivid person. He lit up a room, and people loved to have him in a group. When our daughter was in day care, Ralph worked in her day care center. During parents' meetings, I would be in one group as a parent, and he would be in another group as a teacher. Our group would be struggling in our conversations and would hear Ralph's group laughing and getting louder and louder.

I was reminded of that experience when we joined our early onset/early-stage support group. The people with Alzheimer's met in one room while we "care partners" met in another. One of the partners said after a few weeks, "We're in here crying, and they are over there laughing and singing. Someone had that group singing last week!" That was Ralph.

A little at a time, that vividness faded, like a photograph that loses color over time. For most of the first five years after his diagnosis, there was Ralph-ness—less verbal, less interesting, but still there in flashes. Even in the nursing home, unable to speak much or do anything else, from time to time he would make funny faces in response to some noise or outburst in the room or in response to a conversation. Now, he is mostly silent and unresponsive.

G

Gratitude

When I first wrote this section, I wrote it in the past tense during a period when I did not feel much gratitude. Nobody feels grateful all the time for this experience—Alzheimer's really does suck! But truly, I have and continue to feel gratitude frequently, all along the way. Sometimes I deliberately make myself think of what I have to be grateful for, and sometimes a feeling of gratitude just comes upon me as a little surprising gift.

Early in the process of living with Alzheimer's, I felt grateful for Ralph and the life we had together. I was able to appreciate him more fully and accept his shortcomings while being grateful for his many good qualities. I knew that he had accepted my "issues" and loved me just the same, and I was grateful for that. I recognized that it was good to have the time to connect with each other and enjoy life and its blessings together, a quality I had to learn from Ralph.

As troubles mounted, I was grateful for the circle of support we had and amazed both at the number of people who helped us and some of the people who helped even though they were not close friends. I was grateful to be part of a church community that shared burdens and joys, where people knew and loved Ralph and told stories about him to new people who joined. I am grateful to have been introduced to the Alzheimer's Association and our support group. I am grateful for the Brigham Alzheimer's team, where we got to develop relationships with doctors, nurses, researchers, and staff. And I am grateful for the good care Ralph receives in his nursing home and the people there who help support me.

I recognize that I have been blessed with sufficient resources, access to information and care, and loving people surrounding me—and that not everyone has all these blessings. I don't want to urge gratitude on anyone. But recognizing and being grateful for what we have has helped me balance the focus on what we have lost.

Grief

What is the difference between grief and sadness? I have looked these up in multiple dictionaries and asked friends. My favorite dictionary, the *American Heritage Dictionary*, describes *grief* as "deep, acute personal sorrow, especially over an irreplaceable loss." It describes *heartache* as "sustained private sorrow," so maybe I should use that term, but I won't. *Sadness* is the more general term referring to feelings which may be deep or come and go. With Alzheimer's, there is enough sadness to go around, so I include both *grief* and *sadness* here and hope they do not overlap too much.

On the Alzheimer's journey, grief is a burden we carry— sometimes lightly, sometimes as a heavy weight—for a long time, through the stages of the disease as we experience loss after loss. This grief is inside me, underlying everything I do: holding things together, leading a meeting, making jokes, doing the shopping, chatting with people, even cleaning the bathroom. Early on, I felt sad from time to time but was less aware of the ongoing grief. Now it seems to have moved in as a constant presence, a feeling behind my eyes, a weight that tires me, a cloud or shadow over the brightest of days.

The grief we in the Alzheimer's community experience seems different to me than grieving from a loss after death. Death is a clear and definite absence of the person lost. Our losses are small, gradual, constant, and anticipatory. When death finally comes, it can seem like a relief, a release of the burden carried for so long. One friend said after her husband died, "I have done my grieving already." But for others, the death of a loved one with Alzheimer's, even when a relief, may bring its own grief over the loss of the physical presence of the person and the loss of the role of caregiver.

Environmentalist Joanna Macy in an interview with Krista Tippett on the public radio show *On Being*, said to not be afraid of grief because "if we can be fearless, to be with our pain, it turns. It doesn't stay static. It only doesn't change if we refuse to look at it. But when we look at it, when we take it in our hands, when we can just be with it and keep breathing, then it turns. It turns to reveal its other face, and the other face of our pain for the world is our love for the world, our absolutely inseparable connectedness with all life."

A friend of mine recently told me, when I said I wasn't sure we should celebrate Ralph's and my fiftieth wedding anniversary, "There is nothing like it, is there?" meaning the loss of a spouse in this way.

"No," I said. "There's not."

I was grateful that she understood. Then I thought, there is nothing like the grief she was living with over her granddaughter's ongoing suffering. There is nothing like an African American mother experiencing racism and seeing it affect her child. There is nothing like losing a loved one to drug addiction. There is nothing like living for years in chronic pain.

Many years ago, when my parents lived downstairs and my father was bedridden with multiple sclerosis, Ralph and I had to be home by ten every night, and on weekends at nine in the morning and four in the afternoon, to get my dad up and put him to bed. Ralph did a lot of the heavy work, and I helped. This schedule limited our life somewhat but became part of our routine. It was basically okay.

A woman I knew slightly at work had a husband who drank too much and beat her, and I used to think, "At least I don't have to live with that." I was talking with her one day and realized that she was thinking the same thing about me.

As our old Catholic relatives used to say, "Everyone has their cross to bear." When I was a kid, we thought that was funny—old people exaggerating. Now I know it is true. So many people I know are living with great sadness, and often I do not even know it until something prompts them to reveal it. Then I recognize that they are living with something that colors their experiences every day. I may not know how their grief affects them, but I know that it does. I have learned through this experience the importance of a quote I read that was attributed to Philo of Alexandria: "Be kind, because everyone you meet is fighting a great battle."

Hope

The Alzheimer's Association has been producing videos each year featuring someone with the disease and titled *A Reason to Hope.* Ralph and I were featured in the first one here in Massachusetts. At the end, I was asked to say something like, "I have reason to hope ..." I knew it would be hard for me, so I acted my way into saying the words, trying to project enthusiasm and optimism. But in fact, I live without hope. For us, there is no reason to hope. Currently, Alzheimer's disease is degenerative, progressive, and incurable.

I know that with funding and research and luck, an Alzheimer's cure or prevention will be developed. I love and am moved by the Alzheimer's Association's ad, "The first survivor is out there now." But for those of us living with the disease now, there is no hope for a cure or even improvement.

I have become somewhat obsessed with trying to figure out what *hope* means. As a Christian, I am taught to have "faith, hope, and love." I get faith and love, but hope? In the time I have been living with Alzheimer's, I have heard three pastors preach about hope, and while they were wonderful preachers, smart and sensitive, I mostly did not find them helpful. The best I could get is that our hope is for the long view. And then there is Emily

Dickinson, with "Hope is a strange invention" and "Hope is the thing with feathers." What the heck is that?

For most situations, even the most dire, there can be a flicker of hope. Living with cancer or drug addiction, racism and homophobia, poverty and war—all have a glimmer that improvement is possible, although it may not be likely in many cases. And, clearly, there comes a time when the cancer patient knows there is no hope or the person of color learns to live with the pain of a racist world. I do not mean that Alzheimer's is worse than those things. As with any disease, there is hope that a cure can be found, and I work toward supporting the goal of "a world without Alzheimer's." But for my husband and others at this point in time, there is no hope—no hope that he will get better, no hope that he will have a good day where he will smile at me and connect with me, no hope that I can bring him something to delight him.

I have found that living without hope frees me to live in the present and experience the moments—whether sad or happy or funny or difficult—as they come. The opposite of hope is not necessarily despair.

Finally, I heard a message I could accept. In the same interview quoted earlier under "Grief," environmentalist Joanna Macy said, "I am not insisting that we be brimming with hope. It's OK not to be optimistic. Buddhist teachings say feeling that you have to maintain hope can wear you out. So just be present. The biggest gift you can give is to be absolutely present, and when you're worrying about whether you're hopeful, or hopeless, or pessimistic, or optimistic, who cares? The main thing is that you're showing up, that you're here, and that you're finding ever more capacity to love this world because it will not be healed without that."

I can do that.

I

Incontinence

Somehow, body fluids never bothered me. Well, to be perfectly honest, when Jesse was a baby, while I was not bothered by changing diapers, I *was* grossed out by snot. I had trouble using the bulb baster thing to suck snot out of her nose when she had a cold and left that up to Ralph. But poop and pee—I'm okay.

When my father was bedridden with multiple sclerosis, Ralph and I did our share of cleaning up poop and pee—and again, even at the large adult level, that did not bother me. Sure, when we had just finished cleaning Dad up and were getting ready to go upstairs to bed and he pooped again, I found it frustrating. But it was not at the grossed-out level; it was more at the "Oh no, now we have to start all over again and I'm tired" level.

I am not suggesting that others should be like me. All of us are grossed out by something. All of us have something we cannot tolerate or that is the last straw. I am just reporting.

When people in our support group started sharing stories of their husbands pooping on the floor or peeing into an open suitcase, I said that would be the signal that Ralph needed to go to a nursing home. But I had forgotten that excrement didn't bother me except as a problem and an inconvenience. So when Ralph started to have trouble getting to the bathroom in time, I went into problem-solving mode, not grossed-out mode. I started buying Depends undergarments. At first, Ralph did not like them and made faces, but I talked positively about the fact that they were just like underpants, and he got used to them.

As his disease progressed, one of the things I learned to pay attention to was access to a bathroom. I had to pay attention to his bathroom needs when leaving someone's house, to know where the bathrooms were in a store, and, later, to have a plan for helping him in the men's room or guarding the door outside.

The last year Ralph was living at home, we went on two trips: a ten-day trip to Italy with our church choir and a shorter trip to visit Ralph's family in California. We were in unfamiliar places, and at night, when Ralph got up to go to the bathroom, he would get confused. So I got up with him sometimes three or four times a night. In Ralph's brother's house, the bathroom was right across from our bedroom. *Perfect!* I thought. But every night, he went into the bathroom and pooped on the floor in front of the toilet or peed into the wastebasket. So every night I got up with him, hoping to steer him in the right direction but often just cleaning up after him. It was exhausting, and more important, it was a clear sign that Ralph would soon have to go to a nursing home.

Instructions

Helping someone with Alzheimer's reminds you how complicated it is to do almost anything. In writing or ethnography classes, a common assignment is to write instructions for a simple task like brushing your teeth. There are many more steps than you think. When you have to start helping someone with Alzheimer's, you have to learn this all over again.

Even in the early stages of Alzheimer's, a person may lose track in the middle of what was once a basic task. "Honey, you have to put toothpaste on the brush." The need to do this is usually a surprise—and not a delightful one. *But he could do that yesterday,* I would think. And he might be able to do it again tomorrow. Or it might be a sign of the next step down.

For us, getting dressed was one of those tasks. All of a sudden (at least, so it seemed to me), Ralph got confused putting on a T-shirt. When you think about it, there are a lot of holes in a T-shirt—four to be exact—and different parts of your body go into different ones. I got used to handing Ralph his shirt in the way he had to put it on or turning it a bit as he worked. To be honest, before I developed this calm, helpful skill, there might have been some yelling of, "What the heck are you doing?" especially if we were in a hurry.

One thing I learned in addition to being specific about the steps in the process is that things have to slow down. Problems got worse when we were in a hurry. It didn't work to say, "Just get dressed. We're in a hurry." In fact, it made things worse. The more pressure, the more confused Ralph got. I had to learn to leave more time for getting ready—time for the different steps in the getting-ready process.

J

Joy

Be joyful though you have considered all the facts.
—Wendell Berry

Walking with Ralph was often an experience of joy and appreciation. This was true for much of the fifty years I've known him. Early in our marriage, after we had moved to Chicago, we were walking down an alley on a cold winter day. The alley was a minefield of dog poop. I thought it was disgusting and was just about to complain about it when Ralph said, "You know what's great about winter? All the dog poop is frozen."

Decades later, when he was working in Somerville both for the city and for the church, walking down the street with him was like a different kind of minefield. It seemed he knew everyone— shop owners and ministers, cops and street people. I would start to tell him a story, and he would be working the crowd. I did not always find this charming!

He kept this quality—in fact, it was even heightened—in the early and middle stages of Alzheimer's. Friends who went for walks with him would tell me how much they enjoyed their time with him. "He appreciates everything!" they would say. "Every flower popping out of the sidewalk, every small child we passed with their dad, the blue sky, the breeze." Ralph took joy where he found it.

He really enjoyed his friends, including his brother. In the early stages of Ralph's disease, his brother would call every Monday morning for a chat. Ralph would happily tell me about these chats when I got home from work. "Dennis is such a good guy," he would say. His first year in the nursing home, the choir went to visit and sing with and to him. When Ralph spotted his friend Keene, his whole face lit up and he kept saying, "What a guy! What a guy!"

Our support group also showed me examples of joy in the moment. We, the care partners, would flip from crying to hysterical laughter in a moment. In the other room, Ralph led the Alzheimer's group in singing. At our parties, we played games—a unique experience, playing games with people in various stages of Alzheimer's. It could get frustrating if you didn't appreciate the hilarity of it all.

Joy is like a bubble, a brief shimmering translucent shape that appears briefly and then—poof!—is gone. When it appears, it is important to accept it and appreciate it. We cannot be joyful all the time, but we can be open to joy when it comes.

Our choir director sometimes says to us, after each breath we choir members take during rehearsals, "Recover." Breathe—recover—breathe—recover. He says our bodies need time to recover after a difficult passage or a long-held note. Joy helps us recover from the difficulties and grief we experience.

Juggling

You toss a ball into the air and catch it. Not so hard. Then you add another ball. Trickier, but after a few tries, you get into a rhythm, a pattern. You can do this. So you add another ball, maybe a banana. Oops! That's a little unexpected and different— different weight, different shape. You adjust and drop the banana. It's a little bruised, but you pick it up and start again. After a  *few tries, you start to get the hang of it, and it seems to be working. Then someone throws a pinecone at you and it all comes tumbling down, splat on the ground—or splat, splat, splat, squish. You sigh. This is going to be hard. But you pick up the balls, the banana, and the pinecone, and you start over.*

As Ralph's Alzheimer's progressed, my life became more and more of a juggling act. Every time I would think we had things under control, something would change, and we would have to develop new strategies. Each change snuck up on us, causing frustration and anxiety and yelling until we saw that we were actually in a new phase and adjusted. Ralph was fine at home— with the household chores, church committees, and friends. Then it seemed like all of a sudden, he could not do the chores or find ways to keep busy. He was fine driving, and then fine driving if I was with him to give him directions, and then not fine at all. He was fine going for walks on his own, sticking to main roads and familiar territory, until he wasn't and was lost for twenty-eight hours, having walked on main roads that seemed familiar eight miles into Boston.

In addition, I was working, and my work changed periodically. First, I did not have much travel; then I had regular travel to the same place so I could develop a routine; then I had only local travel, but sometimes I had to be home late or stay overnight when Ralph was getting worse. In addition, my mother was usually fine on her own, but her unexpected hospitalizations, although infrequent, threw off our daily routines.

Piecing things together for Ralph to do was a lot of work, like when tweens are too old for day care and too young to work. Finding activities, organizing ways to get him to them, making sure things were engaging and safe—all seemed like a lot to do on top of working full time. Looking back, it might not have been more than arranging childcare and activities, a task that also changes over time. I guess I had forgotten what that was like, but when Jesse was little, Ralph shared the care (some years doing most of it), and my parents cared for her after school since they were always home, since my father was bedridden with multiple sclerosis. I know some people struggling with younger-onset Alzheimer's who have children and teenagers, some with their own special-care needs. Their juggling is much more than I ever had to deal with.

Each time something changed, Ralph was unlearning things or becoming more and more incapable. That meant more for me to take on. I needed to keep working to support our family, and my work involved a certain amount of travel, often flying to different parts of the country. Every trip involved lots of arrangements, and I developed elaborate schedules for the days I was gone, both for Ralph and for my mother. Things were easiest when I could develop a routine. For a few years, I had a regular trip to Nashville. Because of the time difference, I could spend two full days in Nashville and be gone only one night. They were two long days, but it worked well for a while, with the help of family and friends.

The day program helped as well, and my mother made sure Ralph got on The Ride in the morning to go there. Ralph seemed fine in the afternoons, either napping and watching TV or spending time with friends, which I arranged. He and my mother had dinner and spent the evening together. My mother used to say, "We do very well together." And they did! The two of them got along well and had different and somewhat complementary disabilities.

Then I got thrown off by having to lead a local conference, which required me to stay overnight for two nights; fortunately, the day program allowed Ralph to stay in their respite care program. As the disease progressed, the schedules became more elaborate, the worry increased, and the juggling seemed faster and riskier.

Kempt

The first time we went to the neurologist who was to diagnose and care for Ralph for several years, the doctor described Ralph in his report as "moderately kempt." I am a person who cares about clothes, and in some circles, I am described as well-dressed. While I never took on the traditional wifely role of keeping my husband dressed, Ralph was always a careful and neat dresser, although less careful about haircuts. (Looking back at photos of him performing weddings, I think maybe I should have paid more attention to his haircuts.)

So this description threw both of us. Afterward, I always paid attention to Ralph's clothes and hair whenever we went to an appointment with this doctor. The word *kempt* also made us laugh for several years.

Keep on Keepin' On

Dory, the fish in the *Finding Nemo* movie who has short term memory loss, says, "Just keep swimming. Just keep swimming" as she encounters predators, gets lost, and deals with other problems. At one point, I thought of this as my mantra, and it kept repeating itself over and over in my mind.

I wrote a poem that seems to have the same theme:

I walk in the heat, putting one foot in front of the other.
At first, I walk firmly, enjoying the walk
and the scenes around me,
sure of where I am going. I feel capable and upbeat.
Then, the day grows warmer, my feet get
achy, my enjoyment lessens.
My feet hurt. Will I be able to finish this walk?
I am hungry. Why didn't I bring an apple?
I am lonely. Why didn't I bring a friend?
I am hot. Why didn't I wear lighter clothes?
I make myself stop thinking
and focus on putting one foot in front of the other.

Laughter

While people usually cry over Alzheimer's, there are many funny things as well, and you have to hold on to them. Recognizing the absurdity in many situations can make you laugh. Over the years, I did not keep a journal, but I did write down funny things from our support group and the nursing home, some of which are scattered throughout this book.

When I attended the National Alzheimer's Policy Forum in Washington, I met two men who were in the early stages of the disease. Both of them, without prompting from me, said, "What we need is an Alzheimer's comedy routine." I agree!

Here are a few incidents that make me laugh:

- Ralph was in a day program, and one day I received the following message from one of the staff: "Are you aware that most days he brings your house phone with him in his coat pocket? He doesn't take it out at all, it's not a problem, and I think it probably gives him comfort—but in case you were ever missing it, that's where it is." With a smiley face!

- One night, everyone in our support group seemed to have a long difficult experience to share, with crying. When

Linda's turn came, she said, "Well, we don't have anything. Things are pretty much the same, and it's fine." She paused and then said, "Well, there was one thing. Last week, Pat called 911 to ask what channel *The Rockford Files* is on."

- Jesse sent me this note one day after going for a walk with her father: "I don't want to forget to tell you—We're in Harvard Square yesterday, and walk by this scruffy guy playing the guitar and singing. Dad makes a beeline toward him, and I start to worry that something weird is about to happen that I'll have to explain. Oh, no—the guy stops playing immediately and says "Ralph! How are you??" How does he know this no-teeth street musician??? Sometimes, I give Dad no credit!"

- Ralph was in the hospital for a few days for some procedure. Because he had Alzheimer's, they wouldn't leave him alone but had a "sitter" who stayed with him. I ran into his room one day and said to the woman sitting there (who I thought was the sitter), "Hi, I'm the wife." Then I looked at the bed; a man was there, but it wasn't Ralph. I turned back to her, and she said, "*I'm* the wife." They had moved Ralph to another room.

- Dorothy's husband, Bob, was moving into the later stages of the disease and had not been responding to anything. He was often unhappy, angry, or short-tempered. Dorothy was driving him somewhere and *Car Talk* came on the radio. Tom Magliozzi (who later died of complications from Alzheimer's) said something funny, and both Dorothy and Bob laughed at the same time. Dorothy was thrilled because Bob had been so nonresponsive for several weeks. Then she ran into the car in front of her. She said it was worth it!

- My friend Sue, who goes weekly to the nursing home, had seen a TV show about using improvisation techniques with Alzheimer's patients. One person who shares a table with Ralph is a sweet women in her late nineties who frequently says, "I want my mother. I want my mother." Sue decided to try out an improv technique with her. She said, "I'll help you go to your mother. How would you like to go? By bus? Or should I call a cab?" The woman paused, not saying anything for a longish time. Then she said, "I don't want to visit my mother."

We laugh when things take an unexpected turn and when things seem absurd. Laughter is a gift to accept. When something seems funny to you, it is! And laughter can help you get through the day.

Losses

There are so many losses. They are gradual and ongoing, and they creep up on you. First, there was the loss of memory. I call the moment when I knew that something was seriously wrong "the Ossie Davis moment." I was listening to the news one morning in 2005 when I heard the news that the actor Ossie Davis had died. Ralph was not in the room, so when he came in, I told him. We had a several-minute conversation about Ossie Davis, the movies he had been in, and his marriage to Ruby Dee. Then Ralph went downstairs to get the newspaper. When he returned, he said, "Hey! Ossie Davis died."

The obvious losses include ability to share new information, remembering where he is and is going, driving, and doing chores. In the Alzheimer's community, we talk about these things all the time and how to deal with them. Ralph was able to go to the store with a list; then the list had to include only three things; then one.

Ralph always did the driving when we were together. He liked driving and I did not. He was fine driving for quite a while (he took a test); then he got lost driving so only could drive with me giving directions; then he stopped when he couldn't follow my directions. I felt that as a loss. When he could no longer work and was home while I went to work, Ralph used to make coffee and bring it to me while I finished getting dressed. In the winter, he would heat up the car for me. I miss those things.

My friend Linda, who has not seen Ralph in his latest stage, said recently, "What I think would be hard is to not hear his voice. Ralph had the most wonderful voice, and I always told him he should be on the radio." She was right. Ralph's voice was warm and caressing. It felt comforting and loving. It was like a pillow or a hug. Now, he does not talk.

What I didn't expect were the latest losses. He used to have the most wonderful smell. I always said that if he died, I would keep his dirty clothes to be able to smell him. Now he doesn't have that smell.

He used to be famous for his wonderful hugs. Now that he is in a chair, he cannot hug. And a year ago, he forgot how to kiss. One of the nurses said, "There are worse things." But I can't think of one.

Lying

I prided myself as a truth-teller for many years. I would not have said out loud that lying was the worst sin, but that was how I acted. I did not lie. I was in middle age before I recognized that telling the truth was sometimes hurtful. I had to learn tact, and more importantly, I had to learn when to just keep my mouth shut and not respond to things. I still did not lie, but I learned to not say everything on my mind.

Alzheimer's sometimes requires actual lies. Telling Ralph he didn't have to go to the day program if he didn't like it was kind of a lie. If he had been resistant, I don't know what I would have done. Some women tell their husband they cannot find the car keys and hope he will forget he wanted to drive the car. In an earlier section, I described a very old woman in Ralph's nursing home who used to say, "I want to see my mother." I would respond by saying, "You will see her soon"—not quite a lie for someone who believes in an afterlife. It seemed to quiet and comfort her.

Recently I saw a form printed by the Alzheimer's Association that had the following phrase on it: "use of therapeutic fiblets." People in the meeting were asking what that was, but I knew immediately—and approved.

Marriage

The year after Ralph went into the nursing home, I had to check my marital status on a form for the IRS. For the first time, it gave me pause. Married? Of course I was married. I had been for fifty years and saw my husband nearly every day.

But should I check single because I live alone in the home I own alone, doing all the chores of everyday living alone? I was clear that I was not a widow because my husband was still alive, but I was clearest that I was not divorced.

I am one of millions of people whose spouse lives in a nursing home. When he entered three years ago, he could walk and talk. Then he had a few seizures, and after that, his brain could not tell his body how to stand or walk. At this point, he also cannot talk. For a while, every so often he would say a word or phrase, and he even made funny faces as a joke. But now he does not communicate at all. This man who loved music does not respond to music. He cannot feed himself.

Marriages go through phases. I can say that for sure after fifty years. There's the honeymoon phase, the conflict phase, the "best years of our life." It's hard to say what phase we are in right now. While I see Ralph nearly every day, he doesn't respond to my conversation. I feed him and talk or sing … and sometimes he laughs at my singing! I miss my husband—the man who was my best friend, my companion, my lover. Ralph is no longer the companion who knew me best of all, who made me laugh and think, who shared chores, and who made daily life an adventure. But he is not gone. We are in a space between phases. I'm not even sure I get to say we've been married fifty years, since the last two have had no communication at all. Is that a marriage? Or something else?

A few years ago, a friend whose husband had Alzheimer's and was still at home said, "He is not my husband anymore."

I was uncomfortable with that at the time, so replied, "Well, he is not a companion or a partner, but …"

She interrupted, saying, "No, he is not my husband, and I am his caregiver."

I knew what she meant. When I feel like that, I feel single.

Once, when Ralph was in the early stage of Alzheimer's, I was reading a newspaper article and asked, "What do you think is the secret of a good marriage?"

He answered, "Patience."

I said, "I don't have much patience."

He replied, "But I do."

Some time later, I asked the same question again, just out of curiosity. He replied, "Be willing to take a lot of crap—on both sides."

Another friend told this story in support group: "We were having dinner in a restaurant, and Steve looked at me and said, 'I think we should get together.' I said, 'What do you mean?' I thought he might want to get romantic. 'We are together,' I reminded him. He said, 'I think we should be committed, like forever.' I reminded him, 'We've been together forty years. We just celebrated our fortieth wedding anniversary.' He said, 'Oh. Well, I made a really good decision!'"

I still feel like we made a good decision too. I feel a strong connection between us, even though we can no longer share memories or experiences. Now, even though he does not communicate, even by look, on the days I don't visit for some reason I miss being with him. I try to think of this as just another phase of life and relationship. I hold on to the times when he makes eye contact or laughs.

A few years ago, after months with no verbal communication, he looked me in the eyes, smiled, and said, "Wonderful." It was a special day—and the last word he ever said to me. That was a day I felt married.

Mixed Messages

As should be clear by now, the messages I have to convey are very mixed. I am never quite sure whether to say how terrible this disease is or how manageable it is. Is it a devastating disease that takes a painful toll on loved ones? Is it something you can deal with if you change your expectations and ways of doing things? The answer is yes—both/and.

Sometimes the message I convey is dependent on the audience. Do I want legislators and businesspeople and the public to understand the difficulties of this expensive, long-lasting disease and its changing support needs? Or do I want to provide encouragement to people with the disease and their caregivers? Is it manipulative to change messages with audiences? I worry about that, but both messages are true and need to be heard.

Money

Ralph took care of the bills for most of our marriage and was pretty reliable about doing that. Around the time we noticed that he had bigger than normal problems, but before he was diagnosed, all the checks bounced, and the bank assessed charges. I looked at the checkbook and everything was totally screwed up. It was unreadable, with wrong numbers and things scratched out. So I said I would start doing the bills. The next month, I paid the bills and screwed them up almost as badly. (I did get better!)

For many people—probably most—Alzheimer's creates huge financial problems and constant financial worries. Even people who are "comfortable" constantly worry as they watch their money fly out the door and wonder how long it will last. Money and deciding how to use it sometimes causes strain and conflicts among family members. I have heard of adult children complaining that the caregiver is spending their inheritance. There are a host of new expenses, and they creep up on you as they change over time. Here are some we experienced:

- clothing—new shoes and shirts and pants that are easy to put on and take off

- incontinence underwear

- medications

- legal arrangements—wills, power of attorney, health care proxy

- day program—Ralph went only three days a week

- transportation to the day program—The Ride, which is part of the Massachusetts public transportation system for disabled people, cost three dollars each way. When we shifted to a private driver, the cost was twenty-five dollars each way.

- a tracking bracelet and its membership fee

- aides to assist with showering (when Ralph started fighting the shower)

- nursing home

Many families experience strains we did not. If the person with Alzheimer's was the main breadwinner, the family loses his or her income and may also lose benefits like health insurance—just at the time when health insurance is most needed. Some families have to sell their houses because their mortgage payments are dependent on the lost income.

As care needs increase, some people have to decide whether to continue working or stay home to provide care. If the person with Alzheimer's can qualify for Medicaid, a nursing home—which many people try to avoid, preferring assisted living or aides at home—may actually be the least expensive option. Rules for government supports change all the time and vary depending on different things, including the individual's circumstances, the budget, and the qualification rules. The process is complicated and worrisome. Because it is so complicated, people need legal advice from experts in elder law, another expense many fear they cannot afford.

Music

Ralph loved music. He always listened to music in the car. He loved all kinds of music, from Bach to reggae. On family trips, we all used to sing in the car, especially camp songs.

He had never sung in a choir because he always played sports in school and as an adult was the preacher in church. In the early days of Alzheimer's, after the church he pastored closed, Ralph rejoined OCBC and began singing in the church choir for the first time. He had a beautiful voice—a rich baritone—and a good ear, although he did not read music. It was a delight to watch him sing, throwing his head back and belting out the songs. He especially loved the old-timey hymns from his days as a Southern Baptist.

In 2008, the year he was diagnosed or about to be diagnosed with Alzheimer's, Ralph went with the church choir to Turkey and Greece, where we sang in several places. We sang in Ephesus in the arena where Paul was stoned, in a small beautifully gilded church, and several other special places. It was a joy!

That same year, Ralph decided to try out for the Christmas Revels. The Christmas Revels is a tradition in Cambridge, a musical celebration of the Winter Solstice, with songs loosely cobbled into a story and a different cultural theme each year. Ralph tried out and was accepted after his audition. That year, the theme was England in the time of Thomas Hardy, and Ralph with his full beard and jaunty smile had a perfect look for the time. It was magical to see him lustily singing. He learned more than twenty songs, and he looked great onstage! But I needed to drive him to rehearsals after he got lost twice, and I watched fellow singers push him into position on stage. He often lost his jacket and boots and came out to the car late and with no outer clothes— not so great during the cold and snowy December weather.

The nursing home had a wonderful music therapist who engaged residents in singing familiar songs, involving people with tactile activities like playing with a rope and using simple instruments like tambourines. We were surprised that Ralph did not respond to any of that. Every so often, Jesse and I would sing songs to him when we were outside on the patio. We tried old Baptist hymns, thinking to tap his deepest memories. No response. However, he did join in our singing twice, once to "Rockin' Robin" (without prompting, he went "cheep! cheep!"

at the appropriate time) and once to "John Jacob Jingleheimer Schmidt" with "Tadadadada." Go figure! After that, nothing.

I still sing to him when I feed him lunch in the dining room and oldies are playing. But I don't expect a response anymore.

N

Nursing Homes

I was in my forties the first time I went to a nursing home. I was visiting my favorite great-aunt who had Alzheimer's. She had been the head librarian in a small city and was very intelligent, with a dry and somewhat acerbic wit. When I visited her, she was sweet and smiling, babbling, and walking around with a doll. I cried all the way home.

My father was also in a nursing home for a little over a year. He had multiple sclerosis, and my mother had cared for him at home with help from an aide during the day and Ralph and me at nights and on weekends. When she could no longer care for him, he moved into a nursing home. Dad was mentally capable but did not talk much or engage with anyone. He stayed in his room, watching TV and avoiding the other residents, most of whom were in various stages of dementia.

When I visited him, it seemed like a lot of people were crying. I understood why he stayed in his room. The nursing home made me sad.

Now that I go to visit Ralph in a nursing home almost every day, I have a totally different take on the nursing home experience. Ralph is well cared for in a nursing home with a very good reputation. I know that we are lucky, and there are others that are not so good. But I also know now that my aunt's and father's nursing homes were good ones. My aunt was happy. My dad wasn't, but he was well cared for and was close to home so my mother could go every day. You have to know what to look for.

My mother paid attention to smells. If there was an unpleasant smell, she would have none of that nursing home. I think the most important thing is the staff, especially the nurses' aides or CNAs. Do they seem busy and happy? How do they interact with the residents—and with each other? But on a nursing home tour, you don't talk with the CNAs, so you can't really judge. I judged primarily by the feel of the place and by what I had heard from people I trusted at the Alzheimer's Association and our support group.

I looked for engaging activities for Ralph, but shortly after Ralph entered the nursing home, he could not walk or talk or engage in activities. I didn't like some of the staff I met on tour, but I rarely see those people. The CNAs are the best, and they are the ones who count because they provide direct care. One of them said to me recently, "You have to think of this as a ministry."

A nursing home is its own world, with its own characters playing different roles and its own ways of doing things. There are good ones and bad ones and everything in between. Most visitors tend to spend time almost solely with their loved one, not interacting with other residents and interacting with staff primarily to ask a question about care or a problem. Because I am there every day, I think of myself as more than a visitor. I make it a point to learn staff and residents' names, to smile, and to be nice to everyone. (This is not that natural for me, and I often find it tiring.)

I want staff to like me so they will give Ralph better care. They have a hard job, and I want to be helpful. With residents, I want to give them some extra attention and also be a positive force in the room.

Making friends with staff makes my visits more pleasant and

also gets paid back when we do experience a problem. One of the residents was a horrible man who said nasty things to everyone, especially the black female staff. While he may have had some kind of dementia, he had a knack for saying targeted things that were hurtful. At one point, this man became Ralph's roommate. When I came in and greeted Ralph with a kiss, he said, "Don't kiss him, he's dead. There's no point in it. He's dead." He said this whenever he saw me, as well as other things I found distressing and have made myself forget. At one point, I overheard a nurse say, "He made the wife cry," and I realized that was me. Several staff, even people I didn't know well, came to me to whisper advice about how to get Ralph away from him and out of his room. I will always be grateful for them.

Recently, I overheard someone say, "There's nothing funny in a nursing home." Boy, are they wrong! Like any community, there are sad things and happy things and lots of funny things as well. There's the guy who says "asshole" at the end of most sentences—"Like punctuation," as one of the aides said. There's the woman who repeats phrases over and over until they suddenly shift. Here's an example: "The rabbi is nice. The rabbi is nice. The rabbi is nice. The rabbi is nice. The rabbi peed his pants." Just as you start to think you'll go crazy if she says that one more time, a curveball comes at you out of the blue. You have to be alert for it.

One day Jennie—who doesn't talk much, and when she does, often complains or yells at people—started playfully poking her aide in the stomach. Then she asked, "You don't mind, do you?" The aide laughed and said no. Then, as the aide turned to help someone else with lunch, Jennie started patting her butt. The aides and I couldn't stop laughing.

Once, after Ralph had been in the nursing home for about a year and spoke only infrequently, Charles, one of the nurses, greeted him by saying, "Good morning, pastor." The staff all know he was a minister and often call him pastor. This time, Ralph did not respond, even after Charles said it several times. Hoping to prompt him, Charles switched tack, got his attention, and said, "Pastor, the Lord be with you." Ralph looked him straight in the eye, paused, and said, "Maybe."

A nursing home can be a place to visit or a community of some sort, and I have chosen to make it one of my communities. During the week, my time there feels like going to work, as I feed Ralph lunch and chat with the staff. On the weekends, Jesse and I sit with the same few people, other family members, and residents, exchanging stories and sympathizing with difficulties. In a sense, the nursing home is just a way station, a resting place before the last journey. But it is also a home for the people who live there. This one is a good place for Ralph as he is now, and I am grateful for it.

O

Obituaries

One of my obsessions is reading obituaries. This may be more a result of getting older than Alzheimer's. I scan for people I might know, either from Somerville or Cambridge, or people who lived in Ralph's nursing home. I scan to find people who had Alzheimer's. I read the opening lines to give me ideas of ways to describe death in preparation for writing Ralph's obit: died unexpectedly, passed away peacefully, departed this life, entered eternal life, went home to the arms of her Savior. (I probably won't use that last one, even though Ralph was a pastor!)

Obits often say the person battled or struggled with Alzheimer's. Ralph did not battle Alzheimer's, although I know others who did. He did struggle some in the earlier stages but was able to cover it up with jokes or by directly admitting that he had trouble remembering what he just said. But for the past three years, he has been passive, not moving or making eye contact. He slid into inaction.

Some obituaries are "just the facts"—dates, family members, jobs. I used to think it was ridiculous to name the parents of an eighty- or ninety-year-old, but someone told me such information is often useful for people tracing genealogies. I am curious about the order in which family members are named. Is the spouse first or not? If not, what does that mean? A woman I knew in the nursing home who visited her long-term partner every day, although they were not married, was listed last as a friend. Cold! Not even a close friend or longtime friend.

Some obits are like curriculum vitae—a record of professional accomplishment, a listing of jobs and notable successes. One I read stretched to two columns. I used to think these were bragging, but when I have read the professional accomplishments of some people in Ralph's nursing home, I found the obituary brought them back to life and introduced me to the life they had lived for a long time.

I am touched by the obituaries clearly written by a loved one trying to convey what the person was like and how much he or she was loved. I enjoy the obits that include humor and small tidbits like "she enjoyed her cats" or "her parties included zany activities."

Obituaries serve different purposes. They notify people beyond the immediate family and close friends of a death. We may not always know whose lives have been touched by our loved one; they may want to think of him or even reach out to those left behind. Obituaries also summarize a person's life and tell a story or at least give a glimpse of a person. The obituary I have drafted for Ralph is short and somewhat colorless, so it may be time to rewrite it.

Overwrought

Ralph rarely became aggressive, as do many people with Alzheimer's. One friend had to lock herself in the bathroom while she called for help when her husband threatened her. Another friend's husband pushed someone in the assisted living facility he was in, and they called the police. The police handcuffed him, which only made him more distraught and aggressive.

Ralph never hit me or threatened me. But in his last year at home, he did sometimes get overwrought. He started getting very upset when taking a shower, which he used to love. He would yell and lash out as the water hit his face, and even when I tried to help by holding the movable shower head so it did not hit his face, he still got upset and yelled at me. Getting dressed got harder and harder as he got more and more confused. He would push my hands away from his clothes or throw his shoes across the room in frustration. I worked on talking calmly and carefully, but after a few unsuccessful tries, I would often get frustrated myself and yell at him.

The incident that sent him first to the hospital and then to the nursing home was the most distressing example of Ralph being overwrought. One night, as we were getting ready for bed, he got upset over something and began ranting and yelling, pacing around the house, and trying to go down the stairs (we lived on the second floor). This went on for hours, and I did not know what to do. I was following him around, talking calmly, and trying to get him back on track. I was positioning myself at the top of the stairs to keep him from going down them and getting outside.

I finally called the national HelpLine of the Alzheimer's Association, and it was the only time the association was unhelpful. The volunteer just kept suggesting distracting him with a board game. He was totally undistractable.

At one point, after he had taken his clothes off, he eluded me and got down the stairs and almost out the door with only his undershirt on. I called Jesse in the first floor apartment, and together we managed to get him dressed and into the car to take him to the hospital. I was afraid to take him alone—afraid he would grab the steering wheel and cause an accident. But he and Jesse sat in the back seat, and she talked to him and calmed him down.

In the hospital, he was angry and agitated. When the doctor finally came in to interview him, he kept saying, "You don't understand. You don't understand. I am a person. I am a person. I am—" (long pause as he searched for the word he wanted) "—good-looking." I had been tearing up, but this made me laugh, which I quickly hid. Ralph is very cute but not exactly "good-looking." After the hours of worry, fear, and distress, a laugh, even with tears, was a welcome relief.

P

Paperwork

Alzheimer's takes a lot of paperwork in addition to logistics and patient care. One of the benefits of connecting with the Alzheimer's Association is that we learned how important it is to put certain legal documents in place early. Wills, health care proxy, and power of attorney are all important for dealing with various incidents. Ralph and I were procrastinating sorts and might have put off contacting a lawyer until it was too late if we had not heard stories about the need for these things to be in place.

Because care for an Alzheimer's patient is so expensive—Ralph's nursing home currently costs $12,000 a month—we applied for Medicaid. I worked with a lawyer on this, and I wonder what people do who cannot afford a lawyer. Everything seemed so complicated, and each request involved multiple steps. It took months, and every time I thought we had completed the process, they asked for something else, some piece of paper that I had to track down. They rejected our application two or three times—then they accepted it, and Ralph could pay just his income to the nursing home, about $2,000 a month. Phew!

Oops! Then we got another request for information—does this come every year?— and I had to start all over again. I had put extra money into his bank account as a cushion, and it was too much to qualify for the benefit. So I had to move it out of that account and into another. I now understand that I have to apply every year and have things set up a little better than before.

Purgatory

Purgatory is a Catholic thing. I have always thought it was one of the best things about Catholicism. It is a place people go when they die who are neither good enough to go to heaven nor bad enough to go to hell for all eternity. If you fit in this middle category, you go to purgatory to work out your sins.

Recently, Ralph had a cold and was suffering from a drippy nose and phlegmy cough. I always hated using the bulb baster thing to clear a baby's nose (see "Incontinence"), but Ralph was so clearly unhappy, I bought one to use on him.

I said to Jesse, half in gest, "This is my purgatory, having to clear Ralph's nose."

She replied, "I thought this all was purgatory, but okay."

Questions

My nursing home friend Pauline used to ask me unanswerable questions in the middle of the dining room, things like, "Do you ever wonder why God lets people go on so long like this?" How can I answer this in the middle of the dining room? Basically, my answer to that one would be "Yes." I might want to talk about this at church or in a support group or over coffee, but not in the middle of the dining room.

There are other questions to deal with that are less unanswerable but still difficult. Now that Ralph is in a nursing home, they come up much more frequently. People who don't see him ask me, "How is Ralph? And how are you?" I usually answer "fine" to both. It is hard to know how and how much to answer. Sometimes I don't really want to talk about it. Sometimes I just don't know how much to say.

My friend Sonia had a great question. I had not seen her in a while, and she asked, "How is Ralph?" When I responded "Fine," she followed up with, "What is 'fine' like now?" I realized that I needed to have a better way to deal with this, either by having a longer answer or finding a way to change the subject.

A very common question people ask is, "Does he still know you?" Friends ask it even after I have said he does not walk or talk. Acquaintances often ask it early in a conversation. I used to be able to say, "He likes to see me and enjoys our visits." But now, I cannot honestly say that, since there is no visible connection.

Here I will categorically say: *do not ask that question.* It is very painful, and how can I answer it? I do not know what goes on in his head at this point. Even if he smiles, which is most infrequent, what does that mean? And now that there is no visible recognition or acknowledgement of me, answering this question honestly makes me very sad. There is really not much to say. Generally, the question is a gauge of severity: how bad is it? If you are an acquaintance, this is really none of your business.

I finally asked a friend, "Why do you ask?" I told her I was not offended, just curious. She said she wanted a follow-up to the cursory exchange to indicate her interest and caring. So now, I try to say a little more and tell friends I appreciate their asking about him.

Here are some questions that are a better indicator of caring and connection:

- How often do you see him?

- How do you spend time together?

- Does he seem comfortable?

- Is there anything you need?

Remembering

The most obvious symptom of Alzheimer's is memory loss. They do not remember what they just said or did. They tell the same story over and over. In the early and middle stages, Ralph could remember people, things he saw in photos, and snatches of songs. Now, in the late stages, those memories are gone.

But Alzheimer's does not just affect Ralph's remembering. He has been "gone" so long I fear that people won't remember him when he dies. At this point, he has been gone from the church for over five years and from city life for more than ten. I have friends who don't know Ralph and others who don't remember much about him. His Ralph-ness has faded; his accomplishments and his presence have receded into the past. His most active years were twenty years ago. Of course, this is true of all who live into old age unless they are able to remain active.

The disease also affects my memories of him and our active life together. It has now been three years since we had any conversation at all and at least five years since we had any interesting conversation. This phase feels like it has gone on for a long time. I look at photos and listen to the interviews we did to try to recall him and what he was like.

Ralph-ness

Many years ago, Ralph received an award for his community activity for racial justice. His friend Ed spoke at the ceremony about "Ralph-ness." Given what I wrote above about remembering, I feel a need to try to describe Ralph and convey his Ralph-ness.

I have described Ralph elsewhere as very smart and articulate, funny and quirky. He was also a warm person and a great hugger. I used to say our marriage held together because he could warm me up when I was cold, which in New England is often. A stocky guy, he looked like a friendly bear. He was optimistic and almost always saw the good side of things.

He had a strong sense of goodness and tried to act on his values. When he was in college, a friend of his was struck by the fact that Ralph would pick up trash as he walked through a park. More recently, a friend said, "I learned about being a good person from being with Ralph." Whereas I tend to act out of fairness and justice, Ralph, who shared those same values, acted out of love and kindness. He wasn't a wimp; he stood firm for his values and acted on them, even when that put him in jeopardy. When he applied for conscientious objector status, we did not know whether or how that would affect his career or any other part of his life, and he was prepared to go to prison if his application was rejected.

As a minister, he had the special knack of preaching sermons that were both intellectually interesting to highly educated people and accessible to people with limited education. He wasn't stuffy—he once served Communion with a hamburger bun and Juicy Juice because he had forgotten to prepare ahead of time and that's all he could find at the corner store on Sunday morning. And once, his secretary gave him a Christmas tie right before the Christmas Eve service, which he immediately put on before he went out to the podium. When he leaned forward to welcome the congregation, the tie started playing "Jingle Bells."

He was naturally tactful, gracious, and outgoing to many different kinds of people. He knew all the street people in Somerville and also could relate to professors and senators. When he worked for the city, he became a confidant to women police officers, young Mormon missionaries, and others who came to him for counseling and support. The Somerville police department gave him an award in thanks for being the only person they could reach in the middle of the night to find a place for someone who became homeless after a fire or to solve some other problem. And the mayor, his boss, used to say, "You're the only liberal I can stand!"

For me, he was my loving partner, my closest friend, my favorite person. I once saw a quote by Brian Andreas in a store that seemed to capture my appreciation for our relationship: "He loved her for almost everything she was, and she decided that was enough to let him stay for a very long time." I miss him.

Reactions

People react very differently to living with Alzheimer's. Some people avoid thinking about it as much as possible. Some are sad most of the time. Some fight a lot and are angry at things that happen that they cannot control. Most do experience fear and a little panic at the beginning and at transition points, when the world seems to shift to something new.

A friend whose wife has beginning Alzheimer's said to me recently, "She could not figure out how to brush her teeth this morning." She was shocked, and I saw panic in her face. I wanted to say, "Oh, so what? That's not a big thing!" But I didn't say that. I remembered those little incidents that were a shocking sign that something big was happening. The "Ossie Davis moment" I describe in "Losses" was like that for me—not a big thing, nothing important, but so different from the expected and "normal."

Most of the books and specialists say that you have to learn to accept what is happening and deal with it as best you can. I mostly agree with that. I struggle to keep sadness at bay and work on figuring out how to deal with problems and losses that occur. A support group friend, Susan, and her husband did a lot of arguing, often over things that were nobody's fault but the disease. We all used to shake our heads and think they should get over it. But arguing was what they did, and arguing in spite of the disease may have been like normalizing their changing life, like the arguing they did before the disease entered their life. Arguing was their way of taking charge, of keeping who each of them was and who they were as a couple. It was active combat against the disease. Not so bad, really.

As I have said elsewhere, my reaction was to try to fix things. After getting angry over something Ralph did or didn't do, I'd realize the disease was causing the problem and shift into problem-solving mode. I was pretty good at that and generally came up with lots of alternatives, some of which sometimes worked. I did my share of crying, but I tried to limit it to the car or the shower and follow the model of the old Astaire-Rogers song that says, "Pick yourself up, dust yourself off, and start all over again." Not a bad rule for life, but I was not always able to follow it.

Lest you think from reading this book that I have handled things well, let me tell you about my mouth. After Ralph got lost, and his disease got disturbingly worse, and my mother died, my mouth broke out in painful sores. I have a tendency to get canker sores in times of stress, so I thought that's what this was. I used to get them a fair amount when I was working, but I have gotten them less in the past ten or so years. I tried to stay calm and accept them, knowing they would go away at some point.

When they had been active and extremely painful for over a year, limiting what I could eat without pain to mostly white soft food and milky coffee, I started asking doctors and the dentist about them. Various treatments did not work. Finally, the second time I asked the dentist, he suggested I go to the Oral Pathology Center at Tufts. The dentist I saw there said he knew what it was and tested specifically for that. The test came back positive for pemphigus, and the dentist sent me to a dermatologist at Massachusetts General Hospital who was one of four doctors in the country specializing in this disease. I was cured after several chemo treatments over a series of months. I had really thought that I was handling things well—and I was!—but my body told me something different that needed attention.

S

Sadness

Living with Alzheimer's is sad. I hope this book shows a more complex picture, because it is also funny, strengthening, and challenging. But make no mistake: sadness is always ready to break out.

Early on in our journey, sadness came and went, like an unwelcome visitor, and sometimes I could keep it from coming in. "Okay," I would tell myself, "it is sad, but it could be worse. He can still do things. He is not in any physical pain. He enjoys life." We had bouts of confidence, joy, and appreciation. Then I would start crying, usually alone in the car, often after holding things together at home.

When I feed Ralph lunch now, I am not usually sad. He is in the end stages of the disease and not responsive to anything. Some days, I am okay with this, and when I am talking with other people—friends who come with me or other people in the dining room—I can keep the sadness at bay. But one day, a friend was with me as I fed Ralph lunch and chattered away, and she asked me, "Are you over being sad?"

"No," I said and started to cry.

Systems

One of the things I wouldn't have thought of is that having Alzheimer's suddenly immerses you into different systems you were not part of before. I realize this is true for most chronic diseases. You start going to hospitals more often—for diagnosis, treatments, testing, and clinical trials. You are there so much, you start to know a little about how things work and what to expect. The doctors and other staff you see frequently, especially in clinical trials; where to park your car, especially in downtown Boston; how much time to allot—all these become part of your world.

The Alzheimer's Association was another world we joined. The support group members became close friends. The staff provided additional support with information, advice, and introductions to other systems.

Day programs, assisted living facilities, and nursing homes each had a system governed by different laws and regulations, operating differently.

To succeed in these worlds you enter, it helps to figure out how they work, who does what, and how and where decisions are made. The nursing home is different from the day program, and our nursing home—which is privately owned and run—is different from a nursing home that is part of a national chain.

Someone

My friend Pauline in the nursing home always said, "Isn't it sad? They used to be someone." Many of the people she refers to are very old, in their nineties and hundreds, but others, like Ralph, are in their sixties or seventies but can no longer talk or move around or do much. One was a school principal; one was a doctor; one was a minister; one was a research scientist; one was a translator; and one was an artist. Some are famous enough that when they die, we learn about them in their obituaries featured in the newspaper.

I try to think that those were their jobs, not who they were. But in fact, it is more than that. When people cannot speak or communicate, we don't know anything about them—what they are thinking or feeling. When they don't eat, is it because they have lost the will to live, or are they just not very hungry that day? When they frown, are they unhappy or experiencing a gas bubble? Each person is still "someone," but who?

Donna can barely talk, but from time to time she says to me, "I like your shirt." She raises her hand for water or help sitting up. Once, when Pauline responded to the hand raised by asking, "How can I help you?" Donna said, "It's personal."

Bill finds ways to communicate using three stock phrases that seem to mean different things at different times:"I can't believe it," "What's the story?" and "Go now."

What does it mean to be "someone"?

Supports

Many people deal with Alzheimer's alone. I am not one of them. As should be clear from these stories, we were blessed with lots of support—some of which came to us without asking, some of which we created out of desperation, and some of which we paid for. It was often hard to ask for help, as we did not want to be a burden to others, but we often found that people wanted to help and didn't know how.

When you are dealing with Alzheimer's, you need lots of support and different kinds of support at different stages of the process. Alzheimer's is a complicated disease that tends to go on for a long period of time and affect many parts of your life. That is one of the reasons we found it hard to ask for help—how long would this last? If we ask people for this now, what will happen when things get worse? In addition, there was help we needed that we didn't recognize we needed.

Information

We really didn't know anything about Alzheimer's. It was not part of our family history. None of our parents or grandparents had had it, so we did not think about it before it happened to us. We needed to know about possible treatments, common behavior and ways to handle it, etc. As described in "Doctors and Diagnosis," the first doctors we talked to were less than helpful. We needed specialists, and we were lucky—thanks to a friend—to make our way to the Brigham and Women's Memory Disorder Group. Those doctors recommended we contact the Alzheimer's Association.

The Alzheimer's Association introduced us to other kinds of information we needed or would soon need, including legal and financial issues that we would have to address. The association offers free information and resources on its website, through workshops, and even in individual consultations.

Emotional Support

As I have said in many places, our families, our friends, and our church all provided support. But truly, the greatest amount of emotional support came from our Alzheimer's Association early-onset/early-stage support group. Partly this is because we are not comfortable asking family and friends for emotional support or crying in front of them. With the support group, everything was on the table.

Our group was for people younger than sixty-five in the early stages of the disease and their care partners. Most were married couples—including a lesbian couple—but some were in other relationships. Two women came with their brothers; one man came with his brother-in-law. One nun came alone, getting a ride from a couple who lived near her. We met in separate groups: Ralph with others who had the disease and me with the care partners. It was a place where we could share whatever was going on without wondering whether we were boring people; where we could cry and laugh; where we could get information and advice. Many people come and go in these groups, so I know they are not for everyone. But I don't know how people survive without lots of support, and I recommend support groups to everyone.

While people did come and go in our group, we had a solid core of regulars who soon became close friends. I don't know what they did in the other room, but we didn't care. We each had time to share what was going on, and it varied quite a lot from week to week. Some people talked at length; others said very little. The first week I attended, I said the f-word, and another member said she was so relieved to hear it! (I did try not to swear after that.) There was often crying.

One week, someone said, "What is going on in that other group? We're in here crying and yelling, and they're over there laughing! They were even singing last week!"

I said, "Oh, that's probably Ralph," and it was. He had started singing hymns with a new friend who had a similar church background.

We didn't have to worry about boring people with our problems or exposing our partner's struggles. When we shared problems, others often had solutions. Some weeks it was hard to hear others' problems—especially when it was a foreshadowing of things to come—but it helped to prepare me for what might be in our future. And sometimes it helped to be able to think, "Well, at least I don't have to deal with that."

Our group had parties, including a Halloween party where

we all came in costumes and played games (playing games with people with Alzheimer's is a unique experience!) and a Valentine's party where we danced to '60s rock-and-roll music. And later, we would convene at our loved ones' funerals.

Logistical Help

There are a lot of logistics with Alzheimer's, including transportation, help with doing various activities, and communication. To help Ralph remember what he was doing, I posted a weekly calendar on the fridge and sticky notes all over the house. These worked for a few years. Some people used an answering machine device where they could leave reminders or other messages.

Transportation was easy for a while—then it wasn't. Ralph could drive for a few years, and after that he could walk most places for errands as well as for pleasure, a benefit of where we live. When he started to go to the day program, we were fortunate to qualify for The Ride, a public transportation system for disabled people. Other people paid drivers to ferry their partner to events and activities.

When we decided we could not leave Ralph alone for even a short time, Jesse found the Lotsa Helping Hands website, and we sent out a call to our church community and other friends to sign up to spend time with Ralph when he came home from the day program. More than twenty people signed up, including some I never would have thought to ask. People volunteered to be with Ralph in the afternoons before I got home from work, going for walks or taking Ralph on errands.

For those of us who are reluctant to ask for help, this tool was invaluable, reaching lots of people without asking directly and giving participants the option to sign on for one or several times or to opt out without hurting our feelings. Other friends found different solutions for companionship in activities, including one who hired people to bike and swim with her very active husband.

Personal Care

As the disease progressed, Ralph needed more and more personal care. I was able to help him with dressing and bathing for most of the time he was at home. Just before he entered the nursing home, he started fighting the shower and getting ready for bed. This nightly struggle was wearing and upsetting.

After several weeks of this, I decided to hire an aide twice a week to come in to give Ralph showers and get him ready for bed. This kept us from having fights. But it only lasted a few months before he moved to the nursing home.

Time

The other day, I told someone we had been living with Alzheimer's for ten years. Then I thought, "That doesn't seem right." It seemed both longer and shorter, so I looked up dates.

I am writing this in 2017. Ralph lost his city job in 2001. Recently our state senator, a friend who worked with him back then, said to me, "Don't you think that incident was the beginning of his Alzheimer's?" It was such a relief to hear her say that, because now I do think that was the beginning—although at the time, we thought it was just a fluke.

In 2005 came the incident that signaled to me that something was seriously wrong. We started the serious diagnosis process in 2008 and joined the Alzheimer's support group then. He was formally diagnosed with "probable Alzheimer's" in 2009. Ralph was at home until April 2014, when he went into the nursing home.

The time we have been living with this disease seems both interminable and short. It is very long if I think of it starting in 2001. But we had many happy and active years after that. It seems somewhat short if I think of the last two or three years when he could not communicate at all.

Okay, that's a lie. It never seems short. Three years with him in a nursing home seems very long. It is longer than any of our friends. But there are others in the nursing home who have been there, in a state somewhat like his, for seven years and more.

Traveling

Many people with Alzheimer's who have resources decide to take vacations or visit family on trips they had been putting off. Traveling presents its own pleasures and problems and requires special planning.

By 2010, when our church choir director organized a trip to Turkey and Greece, Ralph had been diagnosed with probable Alzheimer's, and the symptoms were clear but somewhat minor. He was still very active and social. He still loved to sing—the choir planned to sing at several venues on the trip—and the trip included many of our friends. Our daughter Jesse decided to go also. It was a wonderful trip. There were small problems from time to time, but between Jesse and me, we handled most of them, and others helped as needed. The problems were small enough that I don't remember them.

What I do remember is that every time we assembled on the bus or as a group, we counted off, keeping the same number the whole trip. Ralph was the last number, 22, and I had to prompt him each time. So the last numbers went, 16, 17, 18, 19, 20, 21 (me) ... and 22. It was very cute, and every time, everyone laughed.

In late May 2013, Ralph and I joined the choir's trip to Italy, and the problems were not as cute. Ralph still looked fine, was still sociable, and still loved to sing. But this time, I knew his disease had gotten much worse, and I felt I had to warn the group of his shortcomings—especially the five or six people who did not know him, but also the church members who did not see him regularly.

I sent a note to the group, which said in part, "As most of you know, Ralph has Alzheimer's disease. In the past few months, his disease has progressed enough that I want you all to know what to expect. Of course, I take full responsibility for ensuring his safety, but I would like to enlist your help to ensure his enjoyment of the trip." I asked for help in three areas:

- **Talking**—"Ralph has increasing difficulty both expressing himself and participating in conversation. He enjoys being around people but may not have much to say or may have trouble finding ways to say what he would like to. He still enjoys it! You can include him in a general conversation with a smile and a nod. You can engage him in one-on-one chats, tell him stories, remind him of what we did that day ... Asking him questions may be fine, but he may not be able to answer them. Don't worry ... just change track and move on."

- **Following directions**—"Ralph has great difficulty following directions—right/left, take off your shoes, etc. If you are in a situation like this, which is unlikely, you can help by pointing or gesturing and keeping your tone even (okay, I'm not so good with that!)."

- **Separation from the group**—"Ralph does not wander ... and I will keep a close eye on him. However, if we get separated, please help him reconnect with me and the group. I may have to ask some men to go with him to the bathroom sometimes."

This worked well, and everyone on the trip was very helpful. The problems came mostly when we were alone in our room—washing and brushing teeth, using the bathroom, taking a shower, having to pack every day. Everything was a struggle, especially in the morning when we were in a hurry and had to pack. One morning, as the group was waiting for the bus, one woman said, "Someone in the room next door to me kept saying, 'Put your towel on the floor,' over and over and over again."

"That was me," I said.

"No, really," she said. "It was unbelievable."

I said, "No, really, that was me."

While each person and trip are different, here are some problem areas we had to plan for:

- **Going to the bathroom**—He's a man and I'm a woman. He had to go into the bathroom alone. Often, the men in a group whip in and out of the bathroom while the women are in a line of a zillion people, each of whom takes a while. Ralph could be out of the bathroom, confused and unsure in a strange place, for several minutes before I got out.

- **Going through security at the airport**—Ralph always wore a belt, and I had to remember to make sure he did not wear one when we flew anywhere. He needed reminders and sometimes help with taking off his shoes and removing things from his pockets.

- **Safety precautions**—Ralph had a medical bracelet and later a Safe Return bracelet. We also carried multiple photos of him and his passport in case he got lost.

- **Airline special needs**— Even without identifying yourself as special needs, you can board early to get settled, and you don't have to say why. You can also call the airlines ahead of time and register as a special needs passenger. We had one problem with that when I checked "upgrade if possible" and I was moved but he wasn't. I had to negotiate a move with other passengers.

Unknown

Alzheimer's is scary because it sends you into unknown territory. What is ahead? Can I handle that? This isn't the life I signed on for!

When most people think of Alzheimer's, they think of the end stage. They don't have many images of people with early- or mid-stage Alzheimer's. One of the major pluses of being involved with the Alzheimer's Association is meeting people in early stages of the disease who are actively lobbying Congress, writing books and blogs, making jokes about their condition, and riding in bike races. It is uplifting to see that life goes on and may even unlock unknown skills and interests, if only for a while.

The caregiver or care partner may also be taking on an unknown role. I never thought of myself as a nurse or caregiver—I was not even a great mother, especially at the baby and toddler stages!—but I have been mostly okay in this role. You never know!

Upside

"There is an upside to Alzheimer's," I said to a classmate at a recent college reunion.

"I believe that," she said, "since I have terminal cancer, and

I have found the upside to that. I don't have to worry about outliving my money."

Some days, it is hard to remember the upside of Alzheimer's, but here are a few positive aspects:

- It takes its own time, so there is time to enjoy each other and life's moments—time to do things you might have put off, time to appreciate things.

- There is no physical pain. There may be emotional pain and sad frustration at losses, but it is not physical suffering.

- You have time to resolve unresolved things.

- You can make up for past unkindness with present caring. (Maybe that's just me.)

- You gain perspective. Why did I get so mad about that dumb thing?

- You can plan ahead for the end-of-life tasks. I have been giving away Ralph's clothes a little at a time—some to Goodwill, some special things to friends. I have drafted an obituary and planned Ralph's funeral, including asking friends to speak at his service.

Maybe that's it. Maybe you can think of others.

V

Visitors

When Ralph first went into the nursing home, many friends and family went to visit him. This was great, as I was still working. They would go alone or in pairs and take him outside, sing with him, or chat. He went into the nursing home in April, and in the fall, our choir director organized a choir visit, where we sang to and with Ralph—he remembered parts of many of the songs we sang in church. He was delighted with this visit, and his delight was apparent to everyone. The choir also sang carols at the nursing home at Christmas, another lovely visit.

Then, visits started to taper off. Ralph did not respond much to people, so it was unclear whether the visits meant much to him. A friend he used to work with—one of the few men to visit—came every six weeks or so for a long time. Ralph loved those visits. But he did react negatively to one person, and she felt rejected, so she stopped coming. I was afraid that would happen to others, or at the very least that he would not respond in any way. I would have to take care of them in the visit. I stopped asking people to go and almost tried to talk others out of going.

There were two exceptions, both named Sue. Sue #1 is a longtime friend who used to take Ralph to a singing group for people with Parkinson's named the Tremble Clefs. She accompanied another friend who does have Parkinson's and suggested that it might be a good activity for Ralph. They went to this group every Monday for several years; Ralph loved it, and the group loved him. He had a better voice than most participants, as Alzheimer's does not affect the voice. When Ralph went into the nursing home, Sue continued to visit him every week and fed him lunch. When I was working, this was a great help, and now that I am not working, it lets me have a day off. I am eternally grateful.

Sue #2, another friend, used to be a social worker. Her mother has Alzheimer's, and she travels to stay with her mother for weeks at a time to give her sister a break. If I were her, the last thing I would want to do when I came home was visit someone else with Alzheimer's, but when she is in town, she also visits Ralph once a week, usually accompanying me, which is a different kind of break—a friend to chat with. When I am not with her, she always sends a note about Ralph, a mini-report as a good social worker would.

I am not just grateful for these two friends—they are the only people I am totally comfortable having as visitors. They know what to expect, what is normal, and what is unusual, both with Ralph and with the other residents and staff. They know some of the characters in the dining room, their good and bad behaviors. They know Ralph. I relax when I know they are there.

With other people who go infrequently, I am less comfortable. I worry about what they will think of Ralph in his current condition. I worry about how they will judge the nursing home and the overall experience. I don't know who would be comfortable feeding Ralph, so I don't suggest that to anyone. At one point, I found myself saying things like, "You really don't have to go. Ralph is so nonresponsive, he probably won't even know you are there."

Recently, I realized that I would become very isolated in this experience and that people would not have a good sense of what he is like now. It became clear to me from questions people asked or things they suggested that they really didn't have a clue what he was like now. And they'd offer to visit as a way to be of support—a kindness I should just accept. So now I simply say, "Thanks. When would you like to come?"

Walkabout

A walkabout is a rite of passage among Australian aboriginal people. A teenager goes on an extended journey that is a transition between childhood and adulthood. Ralph's transition walk was a transition of a different kind.

Ralph was a walker. He loved to walk around the city. It was something he could do as his disease progressed, and it was something friends could do with him. He went for walks nearly every day and stayed on main streets, comfortable knowing where he was. He was not a "wanderer" who tried to leave the house all the time and had to be tricked into not doing so. He would go for his walk and then come home. He never got lost. Until he did.

In late June 2013, my mother had been in the hospital, and when she came home, she asked me to help her pay her bills. I left Ralph upstairs while I went downstairs to help her. When I finished after about thirty minutes and went upstairs, Ralph was gone, and the front door was open. I figured he went for a walk ... but usually he told me he was going. A few hours later, he was still not home, so I called the police.

In some places, the police would have to wait forty-eight hours to search for a missing adult, but Massachusetts has a Silver

Alert law that lets them look for someone with Alzheimer's right away. The young cop who came to the door was very nice, asked where Ralph usually walked, and went out to look. He also took a picture, scanned it into his phone using the computer in his car, and sent it out to other cops in both Somerville and Cambridge. I was really not worried.

He came back a short time later to say, "There's a beer festival in Davis Square. Might he be there in the crowd?"

Yes! I thought. *He is definitely there—Ralph loves beer!* But no cops on patrol at the festival saw him.

This young officer checked in with me every hour. At one point, he said he had gone to the station and some of the older cops knew Ralph, and they told him what a good guy Ralph was. I was reassured that they were on the case.

At this point, I sent e-mails to people in the area who could look out for him and to our support group, just to let them know. My sister and sister-in-law drove around, and my neighbor and another friend rode bikes around the neighborhood. Then it got dark and started to rain. By this time, I was really worried. Jesse and I drove around—we had not wanted to leave the house before, but it was a last ditch effort. We returned home and went to bed, but neither of us slept much.

In the morning, things got more intense. We did not know what more to do, but the doorbell rang, and our then-pastor Meg and friend Nancy turned up with coffee and computers. I hadn't called them; they just showed up, and I was so grateful. Meg got online and sent notes out to our church members and to other churches in our area and denomination. I called the Alzheimer's Association, and its media team sent out alerts to TV stations.

We got a report from the police that Ralph might have been sighted in Kenmore Square, which seemed unlikely, but Nancy drove me down there to look around the streets and go into hotels. No sighting. We also stopped and talked with the Cambridge police who were stationed at numerous construction sites, and all of them had Ralph's photo on their phones. We checked in with our church in Harvard Square and they had made posters, which were posted around the city by church members and Spare Change vendors (whose office was in our church).

Finally, we returned home. By now, it had been almost a full day. I did not know what else to do.

The next cop who came to the door was a woman who was an old friend of Ralph's. She said, "Don't worry. We will find him." She told me that the deputy chief had taken Ralph's posters down to the Esplanade—even though he was not supposed to go out of the city, she said—and given them to the Boston police who were setting up for the July 4 fireworks.

Meanwhile, our support group was checking in via e-mail, and people were calling. Jesse took the calls. I was grateful for e-mail because it was exhausting to tell people the same story over and over, and because it kept the line mostly free. But then I got a phone call that was really upsetting. A woman called from a nearby elder services organization to tell me that they had to investigate me to determine whether I had been negligent in Ralph's care. She started the conversation by explaining that she was not from our local elder services organization, because Ralph was at that time on its board. So I was really not getting why she was calling. When I finally did get it, I was stunned and upset. Ralph was still missing, and we did not know if he was dead or injured. I was distraught. She kept explaining that it was the law, and she had to make an appointment to come to the house and talk to me. We made the appointment. (Later, when she came, I was cleared of wrong-doing. I understood that she was following the law, but thought she could have been more sensitive in her approach.)

A little after five that evening, over twenty-eight hours after Ralph had left, my brother-in-law Dennis called from California. We had not posted anything on Facebook because we did not want to worry the Hergerts, who could not do anything being so far away. But someone trying to be helpful had posted a notice on their Facebook page, and Dennis saw it. I told him what was happening, and he said that if Ralph was not found soon, he was getting on a plane and coming east to be with us.

Almost as soon as he hung up, our neighbors called to say their daughter, a nurse at Massachusetts General Hospital (MGH), thought Ralph had just been brought in. They were not positive, but a few minutes later, I got a phone call from the Medi-Alert people (Ralph had a bracelet) who linked us in to MGH. He was found! He seemed all right except for dehydration, and we could come and get him.

I called Dennis back, and I also called Pastor Meg so she could send out a note to people. But Meg came to the hospital with Jesse and me instead. When Jesse, Meg, and I saw Ralph, we all went to hug him. He looked up, smiled, and then greeted Meg with a happy hug. (Not me!) And that was the end of Ralph's excellent adventure.

This experience signaled that Ralph could no longer spend much, if any, time alone, and I was still working. Ralph would get home from Rogerson House around three or four in the afternoon, so I tried to be home by then, but it was not always possible. We set up an account with Lotsa Helping Hands and asked friends and family to sign up to spend time with him.

Words

Nursing homes and probably other facilities introduce you to a new vocabulary. We say *residents*, not *patients*, and *aggressive*, not *violent*. One of my new favorites, which I saw in Alzheimer's Association documents, is *therapeutic fiblet* (see "Lying"). These are good words and help you and the staff think of people and experiences in more positive ways.

There are other words people use that are not so benign.

Ralph's nursing home roommate called him "dead" (as described in "Nursing Homes"). My friend Dorothy, whose husband, Bob, had Alzheimer's, told me that a family member once said to her, "Bob is our Forrest Gump." Dorothy was furious about that.

Someone else described a friend of his who "blew out his brains on drugs" as a "vegetable" who spent his days walking the streets.

My heart stopped beating, but I tried to confront it obliquely by saying, "Not many vegetables walk around the street."

He said, "No, I mean, he can't even talk."

Then I did confront it directly and said, "Oh, you mean like Ralph?"

He said no and kept going with his story. I cried for two days over that. I knew that he did not make the connection to Ralph, at least not consciously. But I kept thinking that he would describe Ralph that way to friends, while being sympathetic—"Oh, it's so sad. He's just a vegetable now." And worse, it put that term in my head as I fed Ralph lunch and saw his vacant stare, his difficulty moving, his clenched hands, his head bent to one side.

I attended a workshop on Alzheimer's where the presenter, a professional who was otherwise a good speaker, described Alzheimer's disease as "unbearable"—twice. There were at least two people in the audience who had been recently diagnosed with the disease. One care partner talked to me after the presentation. I mentioned that my husband had the disease, and I told her, "This disease is *not* unbearable. It is difficult. You will need a lot of support, and you can get some of that support from the Alzheimer's Association. But it is not unbearable. You can bear it." I don't know if she believed me, but I hope later on that message will help her.

Words are important. These experiences and my reactions to them have taught me that. Now when I start to think that someone is being too sensitive or I hear others complain about "political correctness" in some area of life that doesn't affect me or them,

I think of my own response to words that hurt me. I realize that what seems "too sensitive" to me may be an especially sensitive area for them, like jumping when someone grabs a bruised arm. I may be too sensitive about Ralph and our situation, but so it is.

Widow in Training

The Alzheimer's folks refer to being a "widow in training." Since the experience is gradual, you have time to get used to being alone, learning new skills, and doing everything for yourself.

Sometimes I feel like a widow already. I sleep alone. I have to learn how to deal with plumbing problems and how to reach out to people when I want company. I give away his clothes, but a little at a time. He needs shirts, but not boots or suits. I remove the labels I had made for his drawers and use the drawers for myself. I plan his funeral. I try to remember him as he was—caring and funny, active in advocating for social justice. I sort through old pictures and tell stories about Ralph and our life together.

Weary

Dealing with Alzheimer's makes me tired. When I was juggling so many things—work and Ralph and my mother and volunteer jobs—I could understand it. I had a right to be tired. But now, I really have no excuse. Some days, the only thing I do is go to feed Ralph lunch. He is not at all difficult, as he eats well and basically just sits there. But often I come home exhausted, and all I want to do is sit and watch *The Waltons* on TV. (This is a major confession, as I rarely have told anyone of this particular "hobby.")

Xmas

Christmas is my favorite holiday, and as an adult, I have always tried to make it as much like a magazine as possible. I like to decorate the house, have an Advent calendar and an Advent wreath, make French Canadian pork dishes, and throw a big—possibly I should say *huge*—party where I make all the food. For several years, I also organized the kids' Christmas pageant at the church.

It was perfect—except when it wasn't. I sometimes tend to go a little overboard and over-romanticize things. I used to get upset when things weren't perfect, and I sometimes overcommitted to doing things that were not absolutely necessary. But with self-reflection, asking for help, and streamlining my admittedly excessive plans, I was able to make Christmas a lovely time.

Still, there were difficulties, and not just because of Alzheimer's. The first year we had our big Christmas party back in the early 1980s, my mother went into the hospital, leaving us to care for my bedridden father, running up and down the stairs while sixty-five guests partied. (After a few hours, I walked around and whispered to a few close friends to get people to leave.) For at least ten years, we juggled three church services—Ralph's church, my church, and my mother's church. And I was working full time while trying to be the perfect Xmas Fairy.

Our Alzheimer's journey can be tracked through Christmases:

- **Pre-diagnosis**—Ralph was getting upset about what Christmas presents to buy. So I told him one thing to get me, something that was usually not available, and he forgot to buy it. I found out ahead of time and ordered it myself. I also got pissed at Ralph.

- **Early stage**—While shopping for gifts, Ralph lost his PDA, the device that helped him stay organized. I went into every store he had gone into, and no luck. I finally had a brainstorm and looked in the bags he had brought home, and there it was. He could still do things like buy presents, and he was still a big help at the party, buying food, working with me to make hors d'oeuvres, and serving as the host.

- **Later early stage**—Ralph and I did all the shopping together because he could not follow a list. It became hard to find things he could do to help, and he was often more in the way than helpful. But he was still the life of the party, welcoming and entertaining our guests.

- **Middle to late stage**—I gave up the party. It was too much work to do alone, with Ralph impaired and Jesse living in New York City. I gave up outside lights, too. Ralph could not figure out how to do it, and I couldn't deal. (I was moved to tears when a neighbor noticed we had not put up Christmas lights and offered to do it.) The last Christmas Ralph was at home, we had guests for dinner, and I served him the turkey leg, thinking he could pick it up with his hands and not need help eating. He could not figure out how to eat it.

- **Nursing home**—Jesse and I fit a visit to Ralph in between church and present-opening. I debate each year whether to get him presents, since he can't open them, but generally I get him something.

Y

Yelling

Okay, to tell the truth, yelling is not new to me or related to Alzheimer's. I was always a yeller, and not in a cute way. I would get mad fairly easily—sometimes about injustice and values that were important to me, sometimes at people who did not do their job or fell short of my expectations or even disagreed with me. At work, I learned to control myself, mostly, but at home I yelled at Ralph. I yelled when he let me down over big things, but I also yelled about smaller things when he did not do things the way I thought they should be done. Ralph did not yell much and generally was much more polite than me.

Once, early in our marriage, we had a big screaming fight. He did yell that time. The argument was about what we would do if we won the lottery. I thought his ideas were selfish and shortsighted; I don't even remember what he thought. All of a sudden, we both remembered that we don't buy lottery tickets and went immediately from screaming at each other to hysterical laughter.

During the "Annoying Period" (see more under "A"), I yelled a lot. Back before he was diagnosed, he forgot the one birthday present I had asked for, and I thought he was not listening or paying attention to me. When he kept losing track of his keys or the car, I got exasperated. When he had trouble doing things he had always been good at, I would sometimes blow up in frustration. I think I experienced yelling as a kind of intimacy and not the rudeness it often was.

When he was finally diagnosed with a disease, I got a lot better. Of course, there was still some yelling. He would yell, "You don't understand how hard this is for me!" And I would yell, "You don't understand how hard this is for *me*!" And then we would cry and hug each other.

Now that Ralph is in a nursing home and does not talk or do anything, I don't yell anymore. I try to make up for my former bad behavior with my actions now, caring for Ralph. Maybe I am a "better person," but basically, I have no one to yell at. I don't yell at people I work with, and I don't yell at my daughter or other relatives.

At the nursing home, there is a resident who is mentally capable but quite crippled and hard to understand. She is a bright and interesting woman, but she can be nasty. She periodically starts screaming things like, "I hate this place!" and "This food tastes like shit!" I am afraid that if I ever am in a nursing home, that will be me—swearing and screaming in frustration.

Z

Zigzag

A friend of mine says this about her mother-in-law: "When we visit her, we never know if we will visit Vicious Vera or Easy Earline." Easy Earline is happy and involved in many activities, walks up and down the hall with her walker, and has boyfriends (!). Vicious Vera gets angry at my friend, accuses the staff of stealing her things, and fights with other residents over those boyfriends.

We did not experience such swings with Ralph. But the disease itself is an uneven and erratic mix of happy and sad, smooth sailing and rocky shoals. I have tried to convey the many aspects of the experience and the fact that the different aspects often collide or follow one another in rapid succession. It is not always good days and bad days, although those happen, but sometimes the good and the bad, the sad and the funny, come on top of each other. Alzheimer's really tests your ability to go with the flow or roll with the punches or deal with lots of different and difficult things.

Zest

What has impressed me more than anything in this long and winding Alzheimer's road has been the zest for life I've seen in most of the people I have met, especially in the early stages of the disease. The people in our support group, the people I met at the National Alzheimer's Policy Forum, and others show more zest for life than most people I see each day. It may be because they know they need to use the time they have.

Many of them use that time to do things they had always wanted to do—take a special trip, learn a new hobby, write a book—and take pleasure in things as they come. Ralph was always an upbeat and positive person, as I have tried to convey in other parts of this writing, but his appreciation for small things, his connectedness with people, and his zest for life carried him through the many early years of the disease.

It is not just Ralph, though. Bruce spent much of his time making jokes. Steve really enjoyed making beer. Eric would happily talk to anyone, even when we couldn't understand a word he said. There were years of joy and pleasure and fun—even though it was mixed with sadness and struggle.

And isn't that life? Every person's life? The mixture is different for different people. The timeline is different. But our experience with Alzheimer's has made me want to use the time I have well, to take pleasure in whatever I can, and to be grateful for all we have been given. That is not a bad lesson to learn at whatever time of life you can.

A quote from Epictetus provides advice I hope to try:
Caretake this moment.
Immerse yourself in its particulars. Respond to this person, this challenge, this deed.
Quit the evasions. Stop giving yourself needless trouble.
It is time to really live; to fully inhabit the situation you happen to be in now.